BLACKS, LATINOS, AND ASIANS IN URBAN AMERICA

BLACKS, LATINOS, AND ASIANS IN URBAN AMERICA

Status and Prospects for Politics and Activism

EDITED BY JAMES JENNINGS

Foreword by Luis Fuentes

Westport, Connecticut
London

Library of Congress Cataloging-in-Publication Data

Blacks, Latinos, and Asians in urban America : status and prospects
for politics and activism / edited by James Jennings ; foreword by
Luis Fuentes.
    p.   cm.
    Includes bibliographical references (p.) and index.
    ISBN 0–275–94746–7 (alk. paper).—ISBN 0–275–94934–6 (pbk.)
    1. Minorities—United States—Political activity. 2. Municipal
government—United States. 3. United States—Race relations.
4. United States—Ethnic relations.   I. Jennings, James.
    E184.A1B554   1994
    305.8′00973—dc20   94–8340

British Library Cataloguing in Publication Data is available.

Library of Congress Catalog Card Number: 94–8340
ISBN: 0–275–94746–7
     0–275–94934–6 (pbk.)

First published in 1994

Praeger Publishers, 88 Post Road West, Westport, CT 06881
An imprint of Greenwood Publishing Group, Inc.

Printed in the United States of America

(∞)™

The paper used in this book complies with the
Permanent Paper Standard issued by the National
Information Standards Organization (Z39.48–1984).

10 9 8 7 6 5 4 3 2 1

Contents

Foreword

This is a timely and important book; the question of how communities of color will relate to each other politically is one of the most important questions facing both activists and scholars in the next several decades. I was part of a social movement in the late 1960s and early 1970s to improve public education in New York City that brought together communities of color and I am convinced, as a result of this experience, of the momentum for social change that coalitions among these communities can generate in order to improve living conditions for all people at the local and neighborhood levels.

At the same time, I am also aware of how easily interests protecting wealth and power can exploit ethnic-centrism in communities of color and can motivate people to fight each other instead of focusing on changing the status quo by challenging the prevalent and domineering systems of power and wealth in the United States.

This book presents a realistic assessment of the problems and obstacles in developing coalitions among communities of color for progressive social action. But it also suggests and cites the principles that could serve to bring communities of color together, in order to move this society closer to the ideals of social justice and equality for all peoples.

Communities of color in the United States have the political potential to generate and revitalize another major movement for social change in this society. But it will be relatively easy for such potential to be derailed by creating conditions that pit communities of color against each other rather than creating an atmosphere where they can work together. Those of us interested in generating social change must ask, therefore, what conditions can lead to communities of color working with each other for common, and progressive, goals? As we work in our respective communities, we must be aware of the potential obstacles—which I believe this book outlines—in order to overcome them.

This book should be read by all activists and scholars interested in changing the face of urban and, ultimately, national America; for if communities of color can come together for progressive political action, then it will only be a matter of time before America finally begins to look like, and act like, what it has been preaching for generations.

Luis Fuentes
Professor Emeritus,
University of Massachusetts

Acknowledgments

This book would not have been possible without the logistical and editorial assistance of several individuals, and support from the William Monroe Trotter Institute, University of Massachusetts at Boston. Tobie Weiner helped me to plan the project and initially contacted and worked with the contributors for timely submission of their draft chapters while I was a visiting Professor in the Department of Political Science at the Massachusetts Institute of Technology. Suzanne Berger, Chair of the Political Science Department at MIT, was also very supportive of my scholarly efforts in completing this book. At the Trotter Institute, Lenora Francis and Lee Kefauver typed early drafts of the manuscript. Gemima Remy assisted me with the final production of the manuscript and also provided invaluable editorial assistance, as did Suzanne Baker. My sincere thanks to these individuals for their professional dedication and support. I also am grateful to Harold Horton and Muriel Ridley for their continual support to the mission and work of the William Monroe Trotter Institute.

Introduction

There are basically three major political and economic systemic challenges facing the American city in the current period. While there are myriad local political, economic, educational, and social problems, it is possible to place these problems into three general categories. These systemic challenges include:

1. Balancing slower economic growth and lower productivity at the national level, with the need to alleviate poverty, and its social effects at the local level;

2. Overcoming incoherent and uncoordinated policy actions, or "tunnel vision" in the making and implementation of public policy in the areas of economic development, social welfare, and human services; and,

3. Resolving and managing effectively social and political tensions between blacks, Latinos, and Asian-descent populations within a context of continuing racial problems at the national and local levels.

This last challenge is particularly important because in many American cities blacks, Latinos, and Asians have an opportunity to develop a political foundation that could support new and innovative policy strategies and human service approaches to these kinds of challenges.

I am proposing in this book, as have a growing number of observers, that a new factor to be considered in urban policy making and local politics in the United States is the emergence of particular political and electoral relationships between communities of color. The future of urban politics and resulting public policy will be shaped significantly by the political posture of blacks, Latinos, and Asians toward each other. Some political scientists have perceptively noted the importance of coalitions at the urban level, and the critical necessity of coalitions for the social and economic advancement of blacks and Latinos. But while a study like *Protest Is Not Enough*, by Rufus P. Browning et al., suggests that the white and liberal sector is critical in such coalitions, it seems to me that in many cities another key political factor will be the state of relations between communities of color.[1]

The nation's major "racial" urban eruptions in the last fifteen years have powerfully raised the issue of relations between communities of color. This was a key issue emerging from the Liberty City rebellions in Miami in the early 1980s, as well as those in Washington, D.C., in 1990, New York City in 1991, and Los Angeles in 1992. There were other factors associated with these urban rebellions, but the political and social impact of the particular relations among blacks, Latinos, and Asians also emerged as a critical question in all of these events.

This book has several goals. Part I includes four chapters that focus on national questions associated with this topic. These chapters place the issue of relations among blacks, Latinos, and Asians within the context of race and urban politics in the United States. These chapters also touch briefly upon the history of relations between communities of color in the United States as well as the possibilities associated with political coalitions between communities of color. It is the hope of the contributors that the chapters serve to inform not only scholars, but more importantly, local and national activists engaged in building coalitions between communities of color.

Chapter 1 presents the argument that the particular political relationship between blacks and Latinos in some cities can represent the basis for changing urban policy in ways that would be more beneficial to people living in the cities. It offers two examples of successful political coalitions between blacks and Latinos: the Harold Washington mayoral campaigns in Chicago in the 1980s, and the community control movement in New York City in the late 1960s. While other groups were involved in these two successful instances of political collaboration between blacks and Latinos, particularly Asians, the coalition between blacks and Latinos in these two cities was critical in the political development of Chicago and New York City.

In Chapter 2, Charles P. Henry examines how relations between blacks and Latinos are a determining factor in the way these groups are becoming politically incorporated in the cities of Miami, Los Angeles, and New York. He describes briefly factors that influence the nature of political relations between communities of color. Such factors include ideology, institutional structures, group size, and relative electoral strength of white liberal sectors.

In Chapter 3, political economist Manning Marable examines a significant racial/ideological obstacle to developing effective political and social coalitions among blacks, Latinos, and Asians. After reviewing the development of strictly "racial identity" politics among blacks, both from an integrationist and a nationalist perspective, he concludes that the class bias of this kind of politics will prevent political collaboration between communities of color.

In Chapter 4, Juanita Tamayo Lott examines the historical origins of the broad political agendas of blacks and Latinos. She also describes how various factors have molded these agendas and discusses the factors that diminish and enhance the possibility of a political coalition between these groups.

Part II of this book includes studies of three cities (Washington, D.C., Miami, and Los Angeles) where the issue of political coalitions among blacks, Latinos, and Asians has been significant in terms of urban politics. These three cities were chosen because they are mentioned and discussed prominently in the other chapters; furthermore, large-scale tensions among blacks, Latinos, and Asians have erupted in these cities. Keith Jennings and Clarence Lusane examine in Chapter 5 the urban rebellion in the growing Latino community of Washington, D.C., in 1990. While they evaluate the policies of black mayoral administrations as a factor in this development, they also look at the institutional and political relationship between the city of Washington and the federal government as a major problem in discouraging the building of effective coalitions between blacks and Latinos. They identify and discuss various factors that could lead to such coalitions.

In Chapter 6 Daryl Harris examines the political and economic relations between blacks and Cubans in Miami. He argues that the issue of race must be analyzed as a critical factor in explaining the particular social and economic relations among blacks, Cubans, and whites. Furthermore, racial tensions have been exacerbated in

Miami as a result of American foreign policy and domestic institutional racism.

In Chapter 7 Karen Umemoto looks at the role of media in exacerbating race relations between blacks and Koreans in Los Angeles. She illustrates how social and political communication between these groups is not only limited, but in some ways confined by the images of and information about each group as presented in the media. She proposes that cultural contact and communication must be part of the strategies for overcoming political conflict between communities of color.

The two chapters in Part III represent an opportunity for the reader to hear the words of two activists, one Chicano, the other Asian, who have spent a considerable part of their lives attempting to build political bridges with the black community in the United States. Daniel Osuna is international secretary of El Partido Nacional de La Raza Unida based in Phoenix, Arizona. His chapter is an excerpt from a presentation made at Michigan State University on February 22, 1993. It is a fascinating presentation focusing on the historical parallels between the Chicano and black communities' political struggles for social equality in the United States. Osuna believes that the recognition and appreciation of this "historical parallelism" can help in building political collaboration between blacks and Chicanos.

It is a very special honor for me, and the other contributors, that Yuri Kochiyama has permitted the publication of a 1972 interview conducted about her work with Malcolm X. Kochiyama outlines how the thinking and activism of her close friend Malcolm X was significant for many Asians living in the United States and abroad. She believes that the kind of philosophy and activism represented by Malcolm X is critical in building political bridges between blacks and Asians in the United States today. In their own way, both Osuna and Kochiyama argue eloquently in these two chapters that the bridges between communities of color can be built and strengthened, as long as they are built on the pursuit, and expansion, of social justice and equality in the United States.

The Conclusion is offered as a way of reviewing some of the ideas presented by the authors of the earlier chapters. It provides a summary of the ideas and models that have been utilized by the contributors, as well as others, to explain racial and ethnic tension in the United States. I also propose two ideas in the Conclusion: first, that the model of "racial hierarchy" is an important one for understanding the nature and future of racial and ethnic tensions among blacks, Latinos, and Asians in U.S. cities. Secondly, as has been argued in numerous of the other chapters here, I propose that the particular relations between communities of color may be one of the critical—if not the key—political factor in determining the kinds of public policies that will be pursued by local governments in responding to growing social needs within an economic context characterized by downturns, recessions, loss of jobs, and a generally somber economic future for the cities in the United States.

NOTE

1. Rufus P. Browning, Dale R. Marshall, and David H. Tabb, *Protest Is Not Enough* (Berkeley: University of California Press, 1984).

Part I

Blacks, Latinos, and Asians within the Context of Urban Politics in the United States

1

Changing Urban Policy Paradigms: Impact of Black and Latino Coalitions

James Jennings

Growing amounts of information and data repeatedly show that blacks, Latinos, and Asians are part of a demographic transformation in this country that has significant political implications for the American city. The possible implications of this population growth will be shaped by the fact that many in these groups experience a greater level of poverty and lower status living conditions compared to whites in the United States. Furthermore, blacks and certain sectors of the Latino population are experiencing increasing social and economic problems that show a need for greater amounts of economic resources, as well as greater priority on urban agendas. Not prioritizing the needs of the growing numbers of poor and working-class Asians, blacks, and Latinos will result in the continued existence of "two societies" in our nation, as has been described in many reports beginning with the Kerner Commission Report. A simple but true statement is that a racial, and now ethnic, as well as class schism in the United States will have negative consequences for everyone in society.

It must be emphasized that despite the commonalities among blacks, Latinos, and Asian Americans briefly suggested thus far, it is inaccurate and ahistorical to present these three groups in ways suggesting that they entail monolithic social, economic, or cultural characteristics and conditions. There is a black middle class, for instance, that although tenuous in terms of its current and future economic status, is different in many ways from impoverished sectors of the black community. And ethnically, the black community is reflecting growing diversity as noted in the number of blacks with birthplaces outside of the United States, particularly in the Caribbean and Africa. Similarly, there are many groups within the categories of Latino and Asian that are different from each other in terms of economic and social conditions, race, language, and culture. Despite these significant differences, however, it is still possible to speak generally of "communities of color" because of racial dimensions in the United States and the fact that, for the most part, whites do stand apart from others in terms of economic and social status. While the economic fate of communities of color is intricately tied to the social and economic welfare of others in American society, these groups now represent a major political factor in determining the kinds of public policies that are adopted by city, state, and national governments to respond to the needs of all citizens.

One possible political scenario in the development of relations among blacks, Latinos, and Asians is an optimistic one for civic activists interested in expanding social welfare and local/neighborhood empowerment programs. In this scenario these groups build and mobilize for common political agendas. This scenario was played out partially in the mayoral campaigns of Harold Washington in Chicago in 1983, the Mel King mayoral campaign in Boston in 1983, and the David Dinkins mayoral victory in New York City in 1989. The Chinatown-Harlem Initiative, a project based in New York City, is another example of the possible outcomes of joint struggles between Asians and African Americans. Historian and cultural activist John Kuo Wei Tchen, one of the founders of the Chinatown History Project, explains part of this organization's mission:

Dramatically changing demographics, well-established pecking orders of ethnicity, race, and gender, and national insecurities about the continued preeminence of the U.S. way of life all conspire to create variations of conflicts and possibilities across the country. The challenge before us is one of long-term bridge-building. Can we forge strong multicultural linkages during the spaces in between the frequent crises which besiege us? Can we begin to change the terms of everyday "common sense" race relations attitudes embedded in the daily occurrence of racial conflict and violence?[1]

These same queries are the focus of many other locally based efforts to develop political and cultural alliances between communities of color. Some of these successful efforts were documented recently in the report published by the Asian American Federation of New York, *Intergroup Cooperation in Cities.*[2]

The relationships that blacks, Asians, and Latinos develop in the larger cities will be critical factors in determining not only the level and degree of social stability, but also the way economic resources are used by politicians and government bureaucrats to respond to the needs of poor and working-class people. Political cooperation among blacks, Latinos, and Asians can help in the development of progressive social agendas that benefit all groups, including working-class whites. There are several examples of this spill-over effect, both in the history of the United States and in the current period. Certainly, the abolitionist movement in this country as well as the civil rights movement are instances where the broad benefits of these periods of social change accrued to many groups and interests.

Another example of how groups of color benefit by supporting each other's political struggles is provided by sociologist Peter Kiang. He reminds us that Japanese Americans' victory in winning redress and reparations recently is a precedent for African American and Native American demands.[3] On a much smaller scale, but still illustrative, we can also point to the issue of police brutality in Asian communities in this country. When the Asian community forced the Boston police in 1986 to open up the internal police misconduct hearings in the Long Guang Huang case, for instance, it was the first time the police in this city ever allowed an open hearing, and it set a precedent for other cases of police brutality to be opened up.[4]

Another possible political scenario in the development of relations among blacks, Latinos, and Asians is a more pessimistic one. In it, we recognize that groups who are economically disadvantaged and growing in number are often posed against each other, sometimes with violent consequences. This scenario would be vulnerable to groups threatened by social change in the United States. The mayor of a big city could attempt to encourage the development of positive intergroup relations; but a mayor could also seek political advantage by utilizing one group as an electoral counterweight to others. This strategy of generating racial and ethnic dimensions in the electoral arena is not new and has strong historical roots in the politics of U.S. cities. Evidence of this strategy was also present at the national level when President Ronald Reagan and the Republican party attempted to mold the Latino electorate as a political counterweight to black Democrats in areas where the latter were particularly strong.

Political scientist John Mollenkopf provides a local example pertaining to the relationships of blacks and Puerto Ricans in New York City:

The numbers of native blacks and Puerto Ricans are stagnant if not declining; population growth comes largely from West Indian and Dominican immigrants, producing conflict over who speaks for blacks and Hispanics. And the most rapidly growing racial minority is neither black nor Hispanic but Asian. Gender differences are also important; most male-dominated occupations are growing slowly or contracting, while female-dominated occupations are expanding. These differences seem to divide and weaken the effort to mount a liberal reform challenge. They also provide the mayor favorable territory for a divide-and-conquer strategy.[5]

The implications for each of these scenarios are significant for the overall politics and economic direction of U.S. cities. If conflict among blacks, Latinos, and Asians is in order for the the 1990s and into the next century, then we cannot expect much progress regarding public policy that responds to the economic and social needs of the poor and working-class stratum in each of these communities. The major reason for this assessment is that the political influence of one group seeking progressive public policies could simply be countered by that of the other group. And as has been explained by Louis Kushnick, director of the Institute of Race Relations at the University of Manchester, the strategy of "divide and conquer," both in the United States and Europe, has been effective in dampening the political consciousness—and therefore progressive activism—of poor and working-class interests.[6] However, if blacks, Latinos, and Asians do support common agendas and coalitions aimed at social change as has been the case in a few instances in American urban politics, then it may mean that the have-nots' interests may be able to develop stronger platforms by which to challenge those representing and benefiting from the economic and wealth status quo in the United States.

There are, of course, many instances of conflict and division between communities of color in the United States, including blacks, Latinos, and Asians. The political relations among blacks, Latinos, and Asians do not generally reflect harmony and common direction. Despite certain kinds of social and economic commonalties, many times these groups are locked in zero-sum political conflict, where one group perceives the victory of another group as a loss for their own group. Despite this sour assessment, there are yet many instances illustrating that important political victories have resulted from coalitions between communities of color. Some of these political successes have produced public policy changes in how a city responds to the broad challenges outlined above. One such coalition occurred in the early 1970s in New York City.

The "community control movement" as manifested in the Lower East Side neighborhood represented a political coalition of Latino, black, and Asian parents seeking to exercise power in the area of public school policies.[7] Led by such educators as the city's first Puerto Rican district superintendent, Luis Fuentes, this coalition struggled against a broad range of opponents, including city government leaders, the Union of the Federation of Teachers, and the major media in New York City. The parents' coalition insisted that parents should have authority to help determine the broad policies molding public schools. Many of the candidates running for the school board in New York City's Lower East Side neighborhoods, and representing the coalition known as "Por los Niños," were defeated in the face of massive resistance and an array of organizational resources from politicians, government officials, and civic leaders. The coalition of parents and community activists, however, did force a debate upon New York City that ultimately resulted in greater attention to the needs and well-being of black, Latino, and Asian children.

The idea of bilingual education did gain wider acceptance and was eventually adopted in different forms in the New York City public school system as a result of the struggles of the coalition in the Lower East Side. And the concomitant idea that the linguistic and cultural backgrounds of children were an important part of an effective pedagogy in the public schools also became more salient in other arenas as a result of the coalition's activism. Another proposal that has become more acceptable, and that was reflected in the parents' coalition in the Lower East Side, is that parents—even in black, Latino, and Asian communities—must be treated as significant partners in the public schooling process. Thus, over a period of just a few years, and despite some electoral setbacks, this coalition of Latino, black, and Asian parents helped to change the general public's thinking about public schools and, more specifically, about how to make schools and school policies more effective in educating children in urban settings.

Another example showing how political coalitions among communities of color can have a significant impact on urban politics and public policy is the election of Harold Washington as mayor of Chicago in 1983. This was an important event not only because Washington was Chicago's first black mayor but also because of Mayor Washington's public policies and political strategy to change the overall social and economic institutional arrangements and direction of one of the biggest cities in America.[8]

This mayor believed that a city can be developed economically within a framework of partnership between downtown developers and the neighborhoods. He believed that it was not necessary to sacrifice the well-being of any neighborhood in order to generate economic growth and to eradicate institutional racism. It was primarily a coalition of blacks and Latinos that allowed the mayor to devise policies and programs that would balance these goals. Although support from the white liberal sector was very important, a critical factor in the mayor's governing coalition was his base of support in both the black and Latino communities of Chicago. Mayor Washington would not have won the election, or reelection in 1987, or have been able to begin instituting a progressive vision of social and economic change for the city of Chicago without the majority of blacks and Latinos and many of their leaders having decided that they must work together in the electoral arena.

As I stated earlier, there are many instances of blacks, Latinos, and Asians fighting each other politically, and the two examples of coalitions described above that did work were short-lived. Nonetheless, these examples can be used to illustrate the potential impact that blacks, Latinos, and Asians could have on the American city through political cooperation in pursuing a progressive social welfare and economic development policy agenda focusing on the well-being of all people.

THE POLITICAL POTENTIAL OF COMMUNITIES OF COLOR AT THE LOCAL LEVEL

The impact of growing populations, as well as worsening economic and social conditions in the American city, may give blacks, Latinos, and Asians the potential political foundation upon which to change public policy in the areas of economic development and social welfare at the local level. The emergence of new political coalitions among these communities of color could represent the basis for conceptualizing and producing different and effective public policy paradigms aimed at resolving the challenges cited in the Introduction. Yet by the same token, it is precisely due to this possibility that some interests may seek to generate, or exploit, divisions among communities of color in the American city.

There are two reasons why these groups are positioned for potential leadership in providing new public policy visions and frameworks that could revitalize the American city. The first reason is simply a matter of numbers. As we near the beginning of the twenty-first century, these groups are numerically dominating the major industrial and high-tech urban centers in the United States. Furthermore, population patterns and birthrates, as well as changing immigration characteristics, in the 1970s and 1980s indicate that these three groups are increasing in size much more rapidly than is the case for European-descent Americans.[9]

The explosive growth of the Latino population, in particular, has created vast political potential for this group. A large proportion of the Latino population is concentrated in nine states that contain 40 percent of all the congressional seats in the United States, as well as three-quarters of all the electoral votes needed to elect a president. While Latinos comprised only 7.3 percent of the total U.S. population in 1985, they were 15 percent or more of the population in the following states: California, Texas, Arizona, and New Mexico. Latinos comprised between 7.5 and 15 percent of the total statewide population in the following states: Colorado, New

York, Florida, and New Jersey.[10] The total electoral votes in all of these states is 169, or more than half of what is needed for a victory (270) to gain the presidency.

It is in some of these places that Asian-descent groups will also have the greatest impact in terms of numerical growth. Over one-third (35 percent) of all Asians and Pacific Islanders in the United States, for instance, reside in California; 9 percent in New York; 5 percent in Illinois; and 4 percent in Texas.[11] Combining the population and projected growth rate of blacks, Latinos, and Asians yields a picture of continuing radical demographic change in the population of several key states and many big cities.

Blacks, Latinos, and Asians, furthermore, continue to suffer disproportionately as a result of pro-growth and austerity state economic policies dominant in the urban United States. These three groups tend to face, to a greater extent than whites, the problems of poverty, inadequate housing, rising crime rates, and drugs, and poor public schooling. Current and traditional approaches to economic development at the local level, whether liberal or conservative, have not resolved these kinds of problems.[12]

It will no longer be possible for these communities of color to "do their own political thing," or simply be absorbed effectively into an expanding economy. The U.S. economy has stopped expanding in terms of productive competitiveness and in the number of jobs that previously could guarantee a group significant social and economic mobility out of poverty or working-class status. Due to a loss of relative economic productivity with foreign countries, the United States economy cannot generate the kinds of jobs it did in earlier periods when the urban-based manufacturing sector, for instance, was healthier. Social and economic problems of the American city have intensified partially as a result of the decline of the manufacturing sector and the rise of a service sector that, in some cases, has resulted in more, but lesser-paying, jobs.

A loss in the investment potential of American business has also occurred, resulting in less wealth to invest in the nation's social, educational, and economic fabric. Political scientist Kevin Phillips reported that, for example, in 1981 the United States was the world's leading holder of investment credit totaling $141 billion, but by 1988 this country had slipped to become the world's leading debtor nation, owing approximately $700 billion. Related to this, he noted that by 1981 the nonfarm productive growth of the country was a record low 1 percent.[13] As pointed out by Phillips, therefore, in a relatively short period the United States has changed from a creditor to a debtor nation. Exacerbating this development are the macroeconomic policies of the nation during the 1980s that will continue to have a long enduring and depressing effect on the nation. Supply-side policies did not encourage investments that would enhance the productive capacity of the nation; much of the capital that was freed by supply-side policies was instead used for speculative mergers and corporate buyouts. It will become harder, consequently, for urban leadership to balance economic growth with the social demands and needs of lower-income and poor populations.

While there have been earlier periods of national economic downturns, of course, it now seems that the current period of downturn may be a new—and possibly permanent—feature of the U.S. economy. As is explained by political scientist Charles V. Hamilton:

The political system is no longer blessed with the economic abundance of an earlier time. Politics in America has been greatly aided by economic resources. This is not to deny or to mitigate commitment to ideology and principle; it simply stresses that such commitments are challenged less in situations of economic abundance. . . . The working partnership of an earlier time between government and the private sector does not seem as promising, at least in the short run. Invariably, this partnership will involve a zero-sum game in the politics of scarcity. Again, pluralist politics is familiar with this, but it has usually had more resources. It would not be an exaggeration to say that . . . the assumptions of pluralist politics in the United States will receive, in the next several years, their most serious challenge.[14]

This picture is reiterated by economist Lester C. Thurow, who argues that it is becoming increasingly difficult for big city mayors to operate effectively under the traditional political parameters and policy frameworks for resolving economic and social problems, in part, because balancing the needs of divergent interests cannot take place in a shrinking or stagnant economy. Thurow captures the essence of a conceptualization that is no longer effective for maintaining economic and social stability.

If we just have more growth, we can have more good jobs for everyone, and we won't have to worry about taking jobs away from whites and giving them to blacks. . . . More is obviously better than less, and economic growth has been seen as the social lubricant that can keep different groups working together.[15]

Within the context of a much smaller and weaker economic state than in the past, it may not be possible to accommodate the basic social, educational, and economic needs of new racial and ethnic groups in America who, like blacks, are expecting to enjoy the fruits of the United States economy.

Due to the broad economic transformation engulfing the nation, we may find that poverty and high unemployment levels for many black, Latino, and even Asian youths will be a resilient fact of economic life in America's big cities. If opportunities for these communities of color to escape mass poverty and economic hopelessness are not facilitated by urban political leadership, however, then it will become more difficult for cities to experience social stability and economic health. The nature, and implications, of these broad economic changes, therefore, cannot be separated from the political query regarding how numerically expanding communities of color will respond to these changes, and to each other.

TOWARD NEW PUBLIC POLICY PARADIGMS

There are generally three broad policy frameworks available to urban political leadership for responding to the social and economic challenges facing cities in the United States. Kenneth M. Dolbeare summarized these approaches as "Cowboy Capitalism," "Yankee Capitalism," and "Economic Democracy."[16] Cowboy capitalism (i.e., conservative policies) is described by Dolbeare as "free market extremism." Its political base is found in the sunbelt region of the country where oil and construction represent major investment resources. Yankee capitalism (i.e., liberal policies) reflects the approaches and interests of the older financial interests that are based in the Northeast and Midwest. While it also relies heavily on the free market, with Yankee capitalism there is an acknowledgment that this must be tempered with the interests of labor and a degree of governmental involvement in social welfare.

These two dominant strategic policy frameworks serve to protect the interests of those groups with power and wealth. The thrust of urban political leadership reflecting either the liberal or conservative counterparts of the same overall strategy for economic development has been to secure benefits for interests that have amassed wealth and power in the American city. The questions that are placed before a city's public agenda by either liberal or conservative policy theorists and scholars are repetitive throughout urban America: How can we attract big business for downtown development? How can the concentration of poor people be reduced? How can we attract the middle class back into the city? How can we build more office space and high-rise luxury hotels for the benefit of the developers and their professional scions? How can we make urban space reflective of those whom we have to attract in order to generate economic development? Which human and social services can be reduced or cut in order to lessen fiscal pressures on those interests with the potential of major capital or financial investment? These are the key questions for urban political leadership reflecting either Cowboy or Yankee capitalism.[17]

These questions have guided the urban political economy in the United States since World War II. The policy frameworks reflecting these questions were facilitated by an expanding national economy. In the current period of declining U.S. productivity, characterized by major demographic changes and continuing racial and ethnic divisions, it does not seem likely that these two traditional policy frameworks can be effective in meeting the social and economic needs of urban America.

There is, however, another kind of potential policy/political framework that may offer greater likelihood of meeting the challenges of the 1990s and beyond, but that has yet to develop a broad political base to sustain it. As stated earlier, Dolbeare has referred to this third approach as "economic democracy." It is certainly conceivable that coalitions between communities of color can represent an important part of the political base for the development and expansion of economic democracy. This is exactly what started to occur during the community control movement in New York City, and the Harold Washington campaign in Chicago. Also, several black national leaders over the years, including Martin Luther King, Jr., and Jesse Jackson, have called for a different and more people-oriented social and economic vision for urban America that seems closer to the school of economic democracy. Many outside the black community have also made similar appeals, as is reiterated in the "Pastoral Letter on the U.S. Economy" issued by the National Conference of Catholic Bishops a few years ago.[18]

Political scientist Marcus D. Pohlmann summarizes some of the policy innovations that urban political leadership might consider under this third approach: constraining the mobility of multinational corporations through "local content" legislation; regulating plant closings; utilizing the power of eminent domain to acquire private property for public use; unitary taxation; worker cooperatives; employee stock ownership plans; and worker self-management.[19] Others have called for full employment policies at the national level, utilization of employee pension funds to increase investments in areas like affordable housing and public education, establishment of basic health coverage as a way to increase worker productivity, greater tax equity policies, and opportunities for worker buyouts of plants that have become unprofitable under current "free market" management. Others have called for more creative and socially responsible use of the billions of dollars in the nation's pensions funds, using the "peace dividend" for social welfare development, and "linkage" policies requiring businesses to compensate the city for social costs incurred in making profits.

This third orientation is not liberal, or conservative, but populist; it calls for an expansion of social welfare, a redistribution of wealth, a rejection of an unrestrained free market, and a rejection of bureaucratic technocracy in favor of expansion of democratic participation regarding economic decision making for neighborhoods, as well as the city. But it would also seek to do this in partnership with businesses and the corporate sector. It is this kind of strategic framework that offers the best opportunity to fight poverty in urban settings, and to do so in ways that discourage racial and ethnic divisions in the city. It is clear, however, that proposed innovations in public policy require a political context for them to emerge and flourish as viable, and eventually be adopted and implemented effectively.

The economic democracy framework calls for urban policies that are more coherent not only within the city and its various social welfare arenas but across cities as well. It would encourage, more pointedly than the two traditional approaches reflecting liberalism and conservatism, a sharing of collective resources between cities and suburbs, as well as greater cooperation between all groups of peoples and neighborhoods. But again, this kind of policy paradigm requires a new political base, as has been suggested by several scholars, including sociologist Fred Block:

While the set of reforms embodied in the alternative growth model do not challenge private ownership of the means of production, they do speak directly to the historic demands of the left for democracy, equality, and improved social welfare. The problem, however, is that in the current circumstances, even a reform proposal that is not anticapitalist appears hopelessly Utopian. . . . [The] pursuit of the alternative model requires political courage.[20]

A few instances across the United States are beginning to show that the creation of a political base for economic and social justice is a possibility and that mutually beneficial political coalitions between communities of color may be a key factor. Thus, as blacks helped to democratize the United States and revitalize its social institutions during the civil rights movement in the 1960s and earlier, today it is the possibility of progressive coalitions between communities of color that may very well be the political glue for saving urban America.

NOTES

1. J. Kuo Wei Tchen, "The Chinatown-Harlem Initiative: Building Multicultural Understanding in New York City," in J. Brecher and T. Costello, eds., *Building Bridges: The Emerging Grassroots Coalition of Labor and Community* (New York: Monthly Review, 1990), p. 192.

2. See Grace Yun, *Intergroup Cooperation in Cities: African, Asian, and Hispanic American Communities* (New York: Asian American Federation of New York, 1993).

3. Correspondence with author, Peter Kiang, professor of sociology, University of Massachusetts, Boston (October 17, 1990).

4. See Elaine Song, *Responding to Anti-Asian Violence in Boston* (Boston: Asian American Resource Workshop, 1987).

5. John Mollenkopf, "The Decay of Reform," *Dissent* (Fall 1987), p. 495.

6. Louis Kushnick, "Racism and Working-Class Consciousness in Modern Capitalism," in B. P. Bowser and R. Hunt, eds., *Impact of Racism on White Americans* (Beverly Hills, Calif.: Sage Publications, 1981).

7. For a summary of this development from the perspective of the parents' coalition see James Jennings, "Community Control: A Grassroots Response," *Journal of Education*, vol. 4 (Fall 1979), pp. 73–85.

8. Abdul Alkalimat and Douglas Gill document and analyze how Mayor Washington attempted to accomplish this feat; see "Harold Washington Becomes Mayor," in Rod Bush, *The New Black Vote* (San Francisco: Synthesis, 1984).

9. See Rafael Valdivieso and Cary Davis, *U.S. Hispanics: Challenging Issues for the 1990s*, no. 17 (Washington, D.C.: Population Reference Bureau, December 1988), Table 1; and W. P. O'Hare and J. C. Felt, *Asian Americans: America's Fastest Growing Minority Group*, no. 19 (Washington, D.C.: Population Reference Bureau, February 1991); also see James Jennings, "Future Directions for Puerto Rican Politics," in *Latinos in the U.S. Political System*, F. Chris Garcia, ed. (Notre Dame, Ind.: University of Notre Dame Press, 1989).

10. Valdivieso and Davis, op. cit.; O'Hare and Felt, op. cit.

11. O'Hare and Felt, op. cit., p. 5.

12. For a critique of these major approaches, and an examination of alternatives ones, see James Jennings, *Race, Politics, and Economic Development: Community Perspectives* (London: Verso, 1992).

13. Kevin Phillips, *The Politics of Rich and Poor* (New York: Random House, 1990), p. 130.

14. Charles V. Hamilton, "New Elites and Pluralism," in *Power to Govern: Assessing Reform in the United States*, Richard M. Pious, ed. (1981), p. 172.

15. Lester C. Thurow, *The Zero Sum Society* (New York: Penguin Books, 1981), p. 17.

16. Kenneth M. Dolbeare, *Democracy at Risk: The Politics of Economic Renewal* (Chatham, N.J.: Chatham House, 1986), see chapter 1 for a summary of these schools of thought.

17. I have raised these questions in the context of several mayoral candidacies in urban America; see James Jennings, "Black and Progress Politics," in Bush, op. cit.

18. See Martin Luther King, Jr., *Where Do We Go From Here: Chaos or Community* (Boston: Beacon Press, 1968); and the "Pastoral Letter on the U.S. Economy," issued by the National Conference of Catholic Bishops.

19. Marcus Polhmann, *Black Politics in Conservative America* (New York: Longman, 1990), p. 226.

20. Fred Block, *Revising State Theory: Essays in Politics and Postindustrialism* (Philadelphia: Temple University Press, 1987).

2

Urban Politics and Incorporation: The Case of Blacks, Latinos, and Asians in Three Cities

Charles P. Henry

In their pioneering study *Protest Is Not Enough*, Rufus Browning, Dale Rodgers Marshall, and David Tabb attempt to develop a theory of urban political change, a theory of political incorporation and policy responsiveness.[1] They argue that the dominant coalitions in these cities have diverse orientations toward minorities and their interests. They attempt a balanced approach using the characteristics of minority mobilization as well as the ideology and interests of the dominant coalition. The work of Browning et al. is especially significant because they attempt to move beyond minority mobilization to develop a theory of incorporation, which for them means achieving something more than getting elected. Minorities must become an integral part of a coalition, according to Browning, and the coalition must be dominant if the interests of minority groups are to influence policy.

According to this theory, three factors shape local mobilization: (1) the size of the minority population; (2) the amount of support for minority interests among the rest of the electorate; and (3) the organizational development and political experience of the group. The theory of incorporation emphasizes the relevance of ideology in making coalitions work to the benefit of minority interests. In particular, the importance of liberal white coalition partners is seen as being essential to minority incorporation.

Browning et al.'s theory of incorporation has been challenged in New York City, where all three conditions are met but minority incorporation has just begun, and in Miami and Los Angeles, where the incorporation of Latinos and blacks respectively has not led to the incorporation of other minorities. These cities provided a significantly broader range of black and Latino groups than the Browning study. Furthermore, each city has a substantial black and Latino population. New York City's black and Latino proportion of the total city's population was 45 percent in 1990, while the proportion for Miami was almost 80 percent, and for Los Angeles it was 44 percent, including Asians.

The examples of New York City, Miami, and Los Angeles introduce a number of additional factors to the incorporation equation. A revised theory of incorporation might include such internal group factors as ideology, interest, and leadership. External factors include city structure, minority population, and the existence of white liberal groups.

NEW YORK

Political scientist John Mollenkopf has argued that New York City contains all the elements Browning et al. cite as essential for minority incorporation.[2] It has a minority population approaching 50 percent. Liberal whites have long been a part of the political scene in New York City. Minority groups are well organized and led by experienced leaders. Yet, it was only in 1989 that New York City elected a black mayor.

Essentially, Mollenkopf cites two factors that have contributed to the lack of minority success in politics. First is the internal problem of racial unity among blacks and Latinos (largely Puerto Ricans). Only 10 percent of New York City's Latinos identify themselves as black compared to 50 percent who say they are white and 40 percent who identify as "other." The issue of racial identification is highlighted by the failure of Herman Badillo to bow out of the mayoral primary in 1977 to support Percy Sutton, a black candidate. Blacks retaliated in 1985 by failing to support Badillo's challenge to Mayor Edward Koch even though there were no strong black candidates. Among blacks, furthermore, West Indians distinguish themselves from African Americans. Geographical differences between the old guard in Harlem and new leadership in Brooklyn is also evident in this city. The second major obstacle to minority incorporation in New York City is the success of white liberals in institutionalizing themselves in the city's large public bureaucracy and labor unions. Their position inside the power structure makes coalition with minority outsiders unnecessary and even threatening.

If black-white coalitions based on the economic interests of blacks and whites from the same class background are impossible because of racial prejudice, then ideology alone is left to sustain coalitions between blacks and whites with different economic interests. When black interests come into conflict with those of liberal whites, as Ralph Sonenshein suggests is the case in New York City, liberal sentiments are not enough to sustain a coalition.[3] In New York City, this conflict has resulted in tension between the black and Jewish communities.

Black-Jewish conflict involves elements of subordination and domination characteristic of the historic relationship between blacks and whites. This relationship is a vertical one in which Jews are represented as storekeepers, landlords, and employers, while blacks are seen as customers, tenants, and domestics. On the other hand, Jews have experienced a long history of discrimination in the United States and were active supporters of the civil rights movement. Thus, they are susceptible to liberal ideological appeals. This presents a different case and set of conditions than a city like Miami.

MIAMI

While 70 percent of the Latinos in Dade County are Cuban, an increasing proportion come from Puerto Rico, Nicaragua, Colombia, and Mexico. These immigrants have settled in a largely uninterrupted string of Latino residential areas, extending west of Miami's Little Havana section.

Miami's black population is also diverse. About 20 percent of Dade County's black residents are Haitian, Bahamian, or Jamaican. However, unlike the Latino population, blacks are dispersed. Moreover, over 60 percent of black Miamians live in unincorporated sections of the county. These settlement patterns are not incidental and have had an undermining effect on political mobilization. When combined with the at-large county and city of Miami elections, the structural barriers to black political participation are formidable indeed. At an earlier stage, Latinos and blacks expressed an interest in changing the at-large system. However, the rapid political incorporation of Latinos during the 1980s has lessened their enthusiasm for this reform.

The black-Jewish conflict that has plagued and continues to plague New York City takes the form of black-Cuban conflicts in Miami. In May 1980 this conflict erupted into violence that took several lives. A Latino man whose car struck an eleven-year-old black girl was seized and mutilated in Liberty City. Black youths halted the car of an elderly Latino butcher and burned him alive. Although most black violence was directed (and reciprocated) toward whites and their property, it is significant that Latinos were not spared.

Like Jews in New York City, Cubans occupy a dominant position in their relationship with blacks. Cubans are represented as store-keepers, landlords, and employers while blacks are the customers, tenants, and domestics. Between 1960 and 1982, Cubans established more than 25,000 businesses of all kinds while blacks owned approximately 3,000 businesses. Interestingly, the poverty so frequently associated with new immigrant groups was absent in the Cuban immigrant community until the arrival of the Mariel refugees from Cuba in 1980.

These class differences loom even larger in the absence of any of the ideological ties that provided some basis for coalition between blacks and Jews in New York City. In sharp contrast to the liberal and very liberal tendencies of New York City's Jewish population, Miami's Cuban citizens are stridently anticommunist and anti-Castro. These conservative views are bolstered by a significant community of Nicaraguan immigrants who are anti-Sandanista. These anticommunist views are strongly held and have played a significant role in local politics. During the sixteen-month period preceding May 1983, the Miami City Commission passed at least eighteen formal resolutions and motions dealing with U.S. foreign policy and expressing their anticommunist views. These views directly collided with the black community when Latino officials snubbed Nelson Mandela during his visit to Miami in the summer of 1990 due to his support of leaders like Fidel Castro.

U.S. foreign policy has also played a substantive role in exacerbating black-Latino tensions in the implementation of U.S. refugee

policy. Approximately 100,000 Cubans departed Havana and settled in the United States in 1980 with about one-third residing in
the greater Miami–Dade County area. These refugees were largely
accepted and assisted in resettling. Simultaneously, about 30,000
political refugees from Haiti arrived in the Miami area from 1978
to 1980. These refugees were denied work permits, refused for food
stamps until 1980, and, with few exceptions, denied access to
medical treatment. Fewer still were granted political asylum. The
official explanation for the difference in treatment accorded Cuban
and Haitian refugees is that the former are "political" refugees
while the latter are "economic" refugees.

The economic clout of the Latino community has also facilitated their rapid political incorporation. Local white business
elites, who have dominated Miami politics historically, did not
feel threatened by the influx of middle-class, business-oriented
Latinos. The white flight that has occurred has not destabilized
Miami's economy. In fact, the Latinization of the economy has
proven to be functional for the major white business interests by
providing the international linkages instrumental to the area's
economic growth. While Miami and New York City are often
cited as examples where communities of color are in perpetual
conflict, some have been more hopeful about Los Angeles.

LOS ANGELES

Los Angeles has generally been pictured as one of the few
success stories in terms of minority political incorporation. Led by
a black mayor for twenty years beginning in 1973, Los Angeles has
avoided the racial polarization that has characterized such cities
as Miami, New York, and Chicago. Political scientist Ralph Sonenshein attributes the success of a biracial coalition to two factors—
liberal ideology and Mayor Thomas Bradley's leadership. Given
the failure of lower-income blacks to build coalitions based on
economic interests with lower-income whites, Sonenshein says
the only option available is a coalition with middle- and upper-
class whites based on liberalism. In Los Angeles a large Jewish
community forms the basis of this coalition along with upwardly
mobile blacks. Unlike New York City, this liberal constituency had
been shut out of city politics until Bradley challenged the white
power structure and those traditional black politicians tied to it.

According to Sonenshein, Bradley was unique in his appeal to aspiring blacks and his contacts with liberal reform organizations like the California Democratic Club.[4] While Bradley has been criticized by both blacks and whites for failing to deliver policy results, the economic growth of the region and Bradley's personal, low-key style have blunted the attacks.

Bradley's narrow reelection in 1989 indicates that the coalition is showing signs of strain. First, the largest and fastest growing racial groups in the city—Chicanos and Asian Americans—are demanding greater political incorporation. It was not until the mid-1980s that Latinos and Asian Americans achieved representation on the city council. Second, liberal whites are showing more concern for the environment and are opposing Bradley's pro-growth policies. Third, Bradley's own political machine has produced black suborganizations capable of challenging and beating his political choices.

While Browning et al. indicate that black mobilization appears to facilitate Latino mobilization, they also point out some basic differences. First, Latinos do not suffer the stigma of blackness, and many consider themselves whites of Hispanic origin. Second, there is greater cultural and socioeconomic diversity among Latinos (such as Cubans, Puerto Ricans, Dominicans, and Mexicans) than blacks. Third, Latinos are more likely to be Roman Catholic and therefore less likely than blacks to see political action as a preferred means of improvement. Finally, Latinos on average have assimilated economically and geographically more rapidly than blacks.

Based on this brief overview of multiracial relationships, we might suggest that blacks and Latinos are the most likely coalition partners followed by Asians and Anglos in that order. Indeed, one *Los Angeles Times* poll supports this ranking. Its survey of Southern California residents found that Anglos were seen as looking least favorably on blacks (44%), followed by Latinos (38%) and Asians (24%). Respondents thought blacks most disliked Anglos (40%), Asians (23%), and Latinos (19%). In fact, the poll suggests that the greatest potential for coalition may lay with Asian Americans and Latinos if attitudes are any guide.

These three brief case studies of multiracial coalitions suggest that ideology, interest, and leadership are internal factors that vary dramatically from city to city. It is impossible to discuss Latinos as an amorphous mass, and even the black population in the United States is more varied than commonly thought. Moreover, class factors play a role not only between blacks and whites, but also between blacks and Cuban Americans and among blacks themselves.

Ideology may be a key that sustains black-white coalitions; however, it may also actually be an obstacle in black-Latino coalitions. Latino immigrants fleeing communist regimes, like their Asian counterparts, oppose liberal, labor-oriented policies like welfare, job security, medicine, social planning, and so forth. The conservatism of the Catholic church is also a contributing factor in their political thought. Finally, many come to the United States without a sense of black contributions to the civil rights struggle and the long history of racial conflict in the United States. These differences make ideological coalition building a difficult task.

Racial identification is also an important factor in political mobilization. Cross-cultural studies of political participation patterns in the United States have produced confusing results at best. For example, some studies report that blacks lag significantly behind white participation rates while other studies have shown the exact opposite. The few studies of blacks, Latinos, and Anglos have not produced consistent results. Moreover, when other forms of political participation (e.g., contributions, campaigning, etc.) or social participation patterns are considered, the picture becomes even more muddled.

In general, these studies have produced two types of theories. Those studies finding less black participation have suggested that blacks are isolated from mainstream politics. Structural obstacles, overt repression, and cultural inhibition are cited as reasons for low black participation. Indeed, from this isolation perspective, any significant increase in electoral activity might be regarded as threatening (negative). Studies showing greater participation among blacks than whites, even when socioeconomic and educational status are held constant, have usually suggested that ethnic community identification is responsible. These studies suggest that blacks compensate for their oppression through increased political and social activity. The ethnic (read racial) community explanation tends to see such activity as a positive development and recent elections involving high levels of black participation have given more weight to earlier research.

To date, there are two possible explanations for differences in black and Latino political participation. George Antunes and Charles M. Gaita contend that higher levels of black participation are triggered by greater perceived levels of social distance held by blacks.[5] That is, when blacks are asked about white attitudes toward blacks, they predict a greater amount of white discrimination than indicated by white responses to questions about their attitudes toward blacks. Chicanos, on the other hand, hold views about white attitudes toward them that are significantly closer to the actual white responses.

Another political scientist, Richard D. Shingles, has provided an important elaboration of ethnic community theory.[6] Although omitting an examination of Latinos, he has cast the social distance explanation in a more proactive direction. Shingles argues that black consciousness contributes to political mistrust and a sense of internal political efficacy which, in turn, promotes policy-related participation. This results in greater political involvement on the part of blacks than whites of comparable status. A later Shingles study found that black men were more active than any other group, even higher status white men. He also finds that, while in 1967 black women expressed higher internal political efficacy than black men, the findings were reversed for 1987.

A second possible explanation for differential rates of ethnic participation may rest in the political climate of each city or region. Sociologist Nicholas I. Danigelis believes that both the isolation and ethnic community theories may be correct depending on the specific political climate.[7] During periods of overt repression visible black political participation may be low with blacks isolated from conventional activity. At times when blacks are receiving some external support, high participation may result in and produce conditions conducive to ethnic community politics. According to Danigelis, a neutral or ambiguous political climate should produce black levels of political participation similar to those of whites.

A political climate theory of minority participation would appear to be a variant of resource mobilization theory. Although resource mobilization has been developed to explain the rise of social movements, it might be particularly useful in minority electoral campaigns that often resemble social movements. Early resource mobilization theorists tended to emphasize the dependence of social movements led by minorities and the poor on external resources, such as sympathetic whites and the press. However, more recent theorists, like Doug McAdam, have focused on the internal factors as well as the opportunities presented by the political system in general.[8] Ronald Walters has applied McAdam's analysis of the civil rights movement to the 1984 Jesse Jackson campaign to demonstrate a class dynamic in the mobilization of support for Jackson in the black community.[9] Walters contends that since blacks were beginning to respond to Ronald Reagan long before black leaders began to consider a black candidacy, the emergence of the Jackson campaign clearly confirmed the thesis that it responded to a popular mobilization already building. While the work of McAdam and Walters tends to support ethnic community theory and corrects an early overemphasis on external support by resource mobilization theory, it does not explain how other elements of the "rainbow coalition" were activated.

The uniform support for Jackson's candidacy across class lines in the black community is generally reflected in the literature on black mayors as well. When Carlos Munoz, Jr., and I looked at black and Latino support, we found high levels of minority support across class lines that tended to support the ethnic community theory rather than the social isolation theory. We also found that less white support for black mayoral candidates may confirm that the black perception of greater social distance between blacks and whites is correct. In addition, less Latino support for Latino candidates may reflect less distrust or lower feelings of efficacy (an earlier stage of political mobilization).

Leadership is an important element in building multiracial coalitions. While it is generally acknowledged that the style and personalities of mayoral candidates are important, organizational links among campaign activists are often overlooked. For example, many of the successful examples of multiracial or biracial electoral coalitions have their roots in ties forged among activists during the civil rights movement and the students' movement in the 1960s. These linkages can often build a sense of trust even when ideological ties are at a minimum. Such ties were absolutely crucial to the Jackson campaign in California.

A good deal has been written on the influence of such factors as the structure of city government, the relative size of the minority population, and the resources of white liberals on minority incorporation. These factors differ from city to city and change over time. In general, it can be said that at-large elections and city manager forms of government work to the disadvantage of minorities. As a minority group approaches majority status it is less likely to look for coalition partners. By the same token, if white liberals achieve insider status, as in New York City, they will be less likely to seek minority incorporation.

Such external factors as U.S. foreign policy and the availability or absence of federal funds for urban development can affect minority incorporation. Cities enjoying economic growth are less likely to encounter resistance to minority gains than those cities dealing with shrinking budgets. For example, blacks are less likely to object to bilingual education programs if they perceive that other educational concerns are also being met.

I have identified a number of factors that should be considered when discussing black-Latino relationships. These include political ideology, economic interest, leadership, governmental structure, group size, and white liberal support. These factors in turn are related to the issue of racial identification and geographical location. Within racial groups there is additional variety as well. In looking toward the future one might expect increased attention to be given to the political incorporation of Latinos and Asian Americans. These groups are the fastest growing in the nation. While whites who are economically secure may not feel as threatened by increased demands from these groups as less secure blacks, they may certainly resist sharing political power.

NOTES

1. Rufus P. Browning, Dale R. Marshall, and David H. Tabb, *Protest Is Not Enough* (Berkeley: University of California Press, 1984).

2. John H. Mollenkopf, *The Contested City* (Princeton, N.J.: Princeton University Press, 1983).

3. Ralph Sonenshein in R. Browing, D. R. Marshall, and D. Tabb, eds., *Radical Politics in American Cities* (New York: Longman, 1990).

4. Ibid.

5. George Antunes and Charles M. Gaita, "Ethnicity and Participation," *American Journal of Sociology*, vol. 80, no. 5 (1975).

6. Richard Shingles, "A Black Gender Gap in Political Participation?" A paper presented at the Annual Meeting of the National Conference of Black Political Scientists, Baton Rouge, March 7, 1989.

7. Nicholas I. Danigelis, "A Theory of Black Political Participation in the United States," *Social Forces*, vol. 56, no. 1 (1977).

8. Douglas McAdam, *Political Process and the Development of Black Insurgency, 1930–1970* (Chicago: University of Chicago Press, 1982).

9. Ronald Walters, *Black Presidential Politics in America* (Albany: State University of New York Press, 1988).

3

Building Coalitions among Communities of Color: Beyond Racial Identity Politics

Manning Marable

Americans are arguably the most race-conscious people on earth. In the United States, "nationality" has been closely linked historically to the categories and hierarchy of racial identity. Despite the orthodox cultural ideology of the so-called melting pot, power, privilege, and the ownership of productive resources and property have always been allocated within a social hierarchy stratified by class, gender, and race. Those who benefit directly from these institutional arrangements have historically been white, overwhelmingly upper class, and male. And it is precisely here within this structure of power and privilege that national identity in the context of mass political culture is located.

To be "all-American" is by definition *not* to be an Asian American, Pacific American, American Indian, Latino, Arab American, or African American. Or viewed another way, the hegemonic ideology of "whiteness" is absolutely central in rationalizing and justifying the gross inequalities of race, gender, and class experienced by millions of Americans relegated to the politically peripheral status of "others." As Marxist cultural critic E. San Juan has observed, "Whenever the question of the national identity is at stake, boundaries in space and time are drawn.... A decision is made to represent the others—people of color—as missing, absent, or supplemental."[1] Thus, whiteness becomes the very center of the dominant criteria for national prestige, decision making, authority, and intellectual leadership.

Ironically, because of the centrality of whiteness within the dominant national identity, Americans generally make few distinctions between "ethnicity" and "race," and the two concepts are usually used interchangeably. Both the oppressors and those who are oppressed are therefore imprisoned by the closed dialectic race. "Black" and "white" are usually viewed as fixed, permanent, and often antagonistic social categories. Yet, in reality, race should be understood not as an entity, within the histories of all human societies, or grounded to some inescapable or permanent biological or genetic differences between human beings. Race is first and foremost an unequal relationship between social aggregates, characterized by dominant and subordinate forms of social interaction, and reinforced by the intricate patterns of public discourse, power, ownership, and privilege within the economic, social, and political institutions of society.

Since so many Americans view the world through the prism of permanent racial categories it is difficult to convey the idea that radically different ethnic groups may have roughly the identical "racial identity" that may be imposed on them. For example, although native-born African Americans, Trinidadians, Haitians, Nigerians, and Afro-Brazilians would all be termed "black" on the streets of New York City, they have remarkably little in common in terms of language, culture, ethnic traditions, rituals, and religious affiliations. Yet they are all black racially, in the sense that they will share many of the pitfalls and prejudices built into the institutional arrangements of the established social and racial order for those defined as black. Similarly, an even wider spectrum of divergent ethnic groups—from Japanese Americans, Chinese Americans, Filipino Americans, and Korean Americans to Hawaiians, Pakistanis, Vietnamese, Arabs, and Uzbekis—are described and defined by the dominant society as Asians, or worst yet, as Orientals. In the rigid, racially stratified American social order the specific nationality, ethnicity, and culture of a person of color has traditionally been secondary to an individual's racial category. But as Michael Omi, Asian American Studies Professor at the University of California at Berkeley, observes, we are also "in a period in which our conception of racial categories is being radically transformed."[2] The waves of recent immigrants created new concepts of what the older ethnic communities have been. The observations and generalizations we imparted to racial identities in the past no longer make much sense.

In the United States "race" for the oppressed has also come to mean an identity of survival, victimization, and opposition to those racial groups of elites that exercise power and privilege. What we are looking at here is *not* an *ethnic* identification or culture, but an awareness of shared experience, suffering, and struggle against the barriers of racial division. These collective experiences, survival tales, and grievances form the basis of a historical consciousness, a group's recognition of what it has witnessed, and what it can anticipate in the near future. This second distinct sense of racial identity is both imposed on the oppressed and yet represents a reconstructed critical memory of the character of the group's collective ordeals. Both definitions of race and racial identity give character and substance to the movements for power and influence among people of color.

In the African American experience the politics of racial identity has been expressed by two great traditions of racial ideology and social protest—"integrationism" and black nationalism. The integrationist tradition was initiated in the antebellum political activism of the free Negro community of the North, which was articulated by the great abolitionist and orator Frederick Douglass. The black nationalist tradition was a product of the same social class, but was influenced by the pessimism generated by the Compromise of 1850, the Fugitive Slave Act, the Dred Scott decision, and the failure of slave uprisings and revolts such as that led by Nat Turner to end the tyranny and inhumanity of the slave regime.

The integrationist perspective was anchored in a firm belief in American democracy and in the struggle to outlaw all legal barriers that restricted equal access and opportunities to racial minorities. It was linked to the politics of coalition building with sympathetic white constituencies that aimed at achieving reforms within the context of the system. The integrationist version of racial politics sought the deracialization of the hierarchies of power within society and the economic system. By contrast, the black nationalist approach to racial politics was profoundly skeptical of America's ability to live up to its democratic ideals. It assumed that racial categories were real and fundamentally significant, and that efforts to accumulate power had to be structured along the boundaries of race for centuries to come. The nationalist tradition emphasized the cultural kinship of black Americans to Africa and emphasized the need to establish all-black-owned institutions to provide goods and services to the African American community.

Although the integrationists and nationalists seemed to hold radically divergent points of view, there is a degree of symmetry between the two ideologies. Both schools of racial identity espoused what can be termed the politics of "symbolic representation." Both the nationalists and integrationists believed that they are speaking to "white power brokers" on behalf of their "constituents" (i.e., black Americans). They believed that the real measure of racial power a group wielded within any society could be calibrated according to the institutions it dominated or the number of African Americans in elective offices. Given the nationwide increase, for example, from 103 African Americans in elected positions in 1964 to over 8,000 in 1993, one could argue that African Americans as a *group* had increased their political power. Any increase in the number of blacks as mayors, as members of federal courts, and on boards of education was championed as a victory for *all* black people.

The black nationalists tended to be far more skeptical about the promise or viability of an electoral route of group empowerment. However, they often shared the same notions of symbolic representation when it came to the construction of social and economic institutions based on private ownership models. The development of a black-owned shopping plaza, supermarket, or private school was widely interpreted as black social and economic empowerment for the group as a whole.

The problem with symbolic representation is that it presumes structures of accountability and allegiance between the blacks who are elevated into powerful positions of authority in the capitalist state and the millions of African Americans clinging to the margins of economic and social existence. The unifying discourse of race obscures the growing class stratification within the African American community. According to Census Bureau figures, for example, in 1967 about 85 percent of all African American families earned $5,000 to $50,000 annually, measured in inflation-adjusted 1990 dollars, while 41 percent earned

$10,000 to $25,000. In short, the number of extremely poor and destitute families was relatively small.

The Census Bureau's statistics on African American households as of 1990 were strikingly different. The size of the black working class and moderate-income people declined significantly, and the two extremes of poverty and affluence had grown sharply. By 1990, about 12 percent of all black households earned less than $5,000 annually. One-third of all blacks lived below the federal government's poverty level. Conversely, a strong African American petty bourgeoisie, representing the growth of thousands of white-collar professionals, executives, and managers created by affirmative action requirements, has been established.

The median incomes of African American families in which both the wife and husband were employed rose from about $28,700 in 1967 to over $40,000 in 1990, an increase of 40 percent. More than 15 percent of all African American households earn above $50,000 annually, and thousands of black professional families have incomes exceeding $100,000 annually. Many of these newly affluent blacks have moved far from the problems of central cities, into the comfortable white enclaves of suburbia. Nevertheless, many of the strongest advocates of racial identity politics since the demise of the black power and black freedom movements come from the most privileged, elitist sectors of the black upper middle class.

The dogmatic idea that "race" alone explains virtually everything that occurs within society has a special appeal to some African American suburban elites who have little personal connections with the vast human crisis of ghetto unemployment, black-on-black crime, rampant drug abuse, gang violence, and deteriorating schools. Moreover, for black entrepreneurs, traditional race categories could be employed as a tool to promote petty capital accumulations, by urging the black consumer to "buy black."

Racial identity politics in this context is contradictory and conceptually limited in other critical respects. As noted, it tends to minimize greatly any awareness of or analysis of class stratification and concentrations of poverty or affluence among the members of the defined racial minority group. This, in turn, limits the capacity of coalition building between blacks and other communities of color. Issues of poverty, hunger, unemployment, and homelessness are viewed and interpreted within a narrowly racial context—that is, as a product of the large racist contradiction within the society as a whole. Conversely, concentrations of wealth or social privilege within sectors of the racial group are projected as "success stories" (see, for example, issue after issue of *Ebony, Black Enterprise,* and *Jet*).

In the context of racial identity politics, the idea of "social change" is not expressed at all. But the current social and economic status quo does not encourage coalition among the have-nots in society. The integrationist generally favors working within the established structures of authority, influencing those in power to dole out new favors or additional privileges to minorities. Their argument is that "democracy" works best when it is truly pluralistic and inclusive, with the viewpoints of all racial groups taken into account. But such a strategy rarely, if ever, gets at the root of the real problem of the persuasiveness of racism—social inequality. It articulates an eclectic, opportunistic approach to change, rather than a comprehensive or systemic critique, informed by a social theory of any kind.

In the case of narrowly defined black nationalism, the general belief that "race" is a relatively permanent social category in all multiethnic societies, and that virtually all whites are immutably racist, either for genetic, biological, or psychological reasons, compromises the very concept of meaningful social change. If allies are nonexistent or at best untrustworthy, or if dialogues with progressive whites must await the construction of broad-based unity among virtually all blacks, then even tactical alliances with social forces outside the black community become difficult to sustain. Even an idea like "Afrocentrism," therefore, may fail to provide that clarity of insight into the contemporary African American urban experience. It looks to a romantic, mythical reconstruction of yesterday to find some understanding for the cultural basis of today's racial and class challenges.[3] Yet that critical understanding of reality cannot begin with an examination of the lives of Egyptian pharaohs. It must begin by critiquing the vast structure of power and privilege that characterizes the political economy of postindustrial capitalist America. Vulgar Afrocentrism looks inward; the new black liberation of the twenty-first century must look outward, embracing those people of color and oppressed people of divergent ethnic backgrounds who share our democratic vision.

Perhaps the greatest single weakness in using the politics of racial identity to serve as a basis for coalition is that it is rooted implicitly on a competitive model of group empowerment. If the purpose of politics is the realization of a constituency's specific, objective interests, then racial identity politics utilizes racial consciousness—or the group's collective memory and experiences—as the essential framework for interpreting the actions and interests of all other social groups. This approach is not unlike a model of political competition based on a zero-sum game such as poker, in which a player can be a winner only if one or more other players are losers. The prism of a group's racial experiences tends to blunt the parallels, continuities, and common interests that might exist between oppressed racial groups and highlights and emphasizes areas of dissension and antagonism.

How do we transcend the theoretical limitations and social contradictions of the politics of racial identity? The challenge begins by constructing new cultural and political identities, based on the realities of America's changing multicultural milieu. The task of constructing a tradition of unity among various groups of color in America is a far more complex and contradictory process than progressive activists or scholars have admitted, precisely because of divergent cultural traditions, languages, and conflicting politics of racial identities—by Latinos, African Americans, Asian Americans, Pacific Island Americans, Arab Americans, American Indians, and others.

Highlighting the current dilemma in the 1990s is the collapsing myth of "brown-black solidarity." Back in the 1960s and early 1970s, with the explosion of the civil rights and black power movements in the African American community, activist formations with similar objectives also emerged among Latinos. The Black Panther party and the League of Revolutionary Black Workers, for example, found their counterparts among Chicano militants with La Raza Unida party in Texas, or the Crusade for Justice in Colorado. The Council of La Raza and the Mexican American Legal Defense Fund began to push for civil rights reforms within government and expanding influence for Latinos within the Democratic party, paralleling the same strategies of Jesse Jackson's Operation PUSH and the NAACP's (National

Association for the Advancement of Colored People) Legal Defense Fund.

With the growth of a more class-conscious black and Latino petty bourgeoisie, ironically a social product of affirmative action and civil rights gains, tensions between these two large communities of people of color began to grow. The representatives of the African American middle class consolidated their electoral control of the city councils and mayoral posts of major cities throughout the country. Black entrepreneurship increased, as the black American consumer market reached a gross sales figure of $270 billion by 1991, an amount equal to the gross domestic product of the fourteenth wealthiest nation on earth.

The really important "symbolic" triumphs of this privileged strata of the African American community were not the dynamic 1984 and 1988 presidential campaigns of Jesse Jackson; they were instead the electoral victory of Democratic "moderate" Doug Wilder as Virginia governor in 1990, and the appointment of former Jackson lieutenant-turned-moderate Ron Brown as head of the Democratic National Committee. Despite the defeats represented by Reaganism and the absence of affirmative action enforcement, there was a sense that the strategy of "symbolic representation" had cemented this strata's hegemony over the bulk of the black population. Black politicians like Doug Wilder and television celebrity journalists such as black-nationalist-turned-Republican Tony Brown simply were not interested in pursuing coalitions between blacks and other people of color—such coalitions do not serve their interests and the agenda of "symbolic representation." Multiracial, multiclass alliances raised too many questions about the absence of political accountability between middle-class "leaders" and their working-class and low-income "followers." Even Jesse Jackson shied away from addressing a black-Latino alliance except in the most superficial terms.

By the late 1980s and early 1990s, however, the long-delayed brown-black dialogue at the national level began crystallizing into tensions around at least four critical issues. First, after the census of 1990, scores of Congressional districts were reapportioned to have African American or Latino pluralities or majorities, guaranteeing greater minority group representation in Congress. However, in cities and districts where Latinos and blacks were roughly divided, or especially in those districts which blacks had controlled in previous years but in which

Latinos were in the majority, disagreements often led to fractious ethnic conflicts. Latinos claimed that they were grossly underrepresented within the political process.

Some African American middle-class leaders argued that "Latinos" actually represented three distinct groups with little or no shared history or common culture: Mexican Americans, concentrated overwhelmingly in the southwestern states; Latinos from the Caribbean, chiefly Puerto Ricans and Dominicans, most of whom had migrated to New York City and the Northeast since 1945; and Cuban Americans, definitely not an "underprivileged minority," and as such not meritting the benefits of minority set-aside programs, affirmative action, and equal opportunity programs. The cultural politics of Afrocentrism made it difficult for some African American leaders to recognize significant common interests with Latinos.

Second, immigration issues are also at the center of recent Latino-black conflicts. Over one-third of the Latino population of more than 24 million in the United States consists of undocumented workers. Some middle-class African American leaders (and even a few Latino leaders, however), have taken the politically conservative viewpoint that undocumented Latino workers deprive poor citizens of jobs within the low-wage sectors of the economy. Third, the expansion and maintenance of bilingual education and services in public schools has also been an issue of contention.

Finally, the key element that drives these debates and tensions between blacks and Latinos is the rapid transformation of America's nonwhite demography. Because of relatively higher birthrates than the general population and substantial immigration, within less than two decades Latinos as a group will outnumber African Americans as the largest minority group in the United States. Even by 1990, about one out of nine U.S. households spoke a non-English language at home, predominantly Spanish.

Black middle-class leaders who were accustomed to advocating the interests of their constituents in simplistic racial terms were increasingly confronted by Latinos who felt alienated from the system and largely ignored and underrepresented by the political process. Thus, in May 1991, Latinos took to the streets in Washington, D.C., hurling bottles and rocks and looting stores, when local police shot a Salvadoran man who they claimed had wielded a knife in a confrontation with them. African American Mayor Sharon Pratt Kelly ordered over one thousand police officers to patrol the city's Latino neighborhoods and use tear gas to quell the public disturbances. In effect then, a black administration in Washington, D.C., used the power of the police and courts to suppress the grievances of Latinos—just as white administrations had done against black protesters during the urban uprisings of 1968.

The tragedy underlying this issue is that too little is done either by African American or Latino mainstream leaders who practice racial identity politics, to transcend parochialism and redefine their agendas on common ground. Latinos and blacks alike can agree on an overwhelming list of issues—such as the inclusion of multicultural curricula in public schools, improvements in public health care, job training initiatives, the expansion of public transportation and housing for low- to moderate-income people, and greater fairness and legal rights within the criminal justice system. Despite the image that Latinos as a group are more "economically privileged" than African Americans, Mexican American families earn only slightly more than black households, and Puerto Rican families earn less than black Americans on average. Economically, Latinos and African Americans both have experienced the greatest decline in real income and some of the greatest increases in poverty rates within the United States. From 1973 to 1990, for example, the incomes for families headed by a parent under 30 years of age declined 28 percent for Latino families and 48 percent for African American families. The poverty rates for young families in these same years rose 44 percent for Latinos and 58 percent for blacks.

There is also substantial evidence that Latinos continue to experience discrimination in elementary, secondary, and higher education that is in many respects more severe than that experienced by African Americans. Although high school graduation rates for the entire population have steadily improved, the rates for Latinos have declined consistently since the mid-1980s. In 1989, for instance, 76 percent of all African Americans and 82 percent of all whites aged 18 to 24 had graduated from high school. By contrast, the graduation rate for Latinos in 1989 was 56 percent. By 1992, the high school completion rate for Latino males dropped to its lowest level, 47.8 percent, since such figures were first collected by the American Council on Education in 1972. In colleges and universities, the pattern of Latino inequality was the same. In 1991, 34 percent of all whites and 24 percent of all African Americans aged 18 to 24 were enrolled in college. Latino college enrollment for the same age group was barely 18 percent. As of 1992, approximately 22 percent of the non-Latino adult population in the United States possessed at least a four-year college degree. College graduation rates for Latino adults were just 10 percent.[4]

Thus, on a series of public policy issues—access to quality education, economic opportunity, the availability of human services, and civil rights—Latinos and African Americans share a core set of common concerns, grievances, and long-term interests, as has been suggested by James Jennings in the Introduction of this book. What is missing is the dynamic vision and political leadership necessary to build something more permanent than temporary electoral coalitions between these groups.

A parallel situation exists between Asian Americans, Pacific Americans, and the black American community. Two generations ago, the Asian American population was comparatively small, except in states such as California, Washington, and New York. With the end of discriminatory immigration restrictions on Asians in 1965, however, the Asian American population began to soar dramatically, changing the ethnic and racial character of many places in urban (and suburban) America. In the years 1970 to 1990, to cite one instance of this growth, the Korean population increased from 70,000 to 820,000 persons. Since 1980, about 33,000 Koreans have entered the United States each year, a rate of immigration exceeded only by Latinos and Filipinos. According to the 1990 census, the Asian American and Pacific Islander population in the United States now exceeds 7.3 million and is concentrated in a few states and major cities.

Some of the newer Asian immigrants in the 1970s and 1980s were of middle-class origins with backgrounds in entrepreneurship, small manufacturing, and the white-collar professions. Thousands of Asian American small-scale, family-owned businesses began to develop in black and Latino neighborhoods, in many instances taking the place that Jewish merchants had occupied in ghettoes a generation before. It did not take long before

Latino and black petty hostilities and grievances against this new ethnic entrepreneurial group began to crystallize into racial animosity. When African American rapper Ice Cube expressed his anger against Los Angeles's Korean American business community in the 1991 song "Black Korea," he was also voicing the popular sentiments of many younger blacks. This kind of sentiment was exacerbated in Los Angeles when a black teenage girl was killed by Korean American merchant Soon Ja Du; although the act resulted in a conviction of voluntary manslaughter, the sentence was only probation and community service.

This sentiment explains, in part, why in the aftermath of the blatant miscarriage of justice—the acquittals of four white police officers for the violent beating of Rodney King—in Los Angeles's federal court in 1993, the anger and outrage within the African American community was channeled not against the state and corporations but against small Korean American merchants.

Throughout Los Angeles, over 1,500 Korean American–owned stores were destroyed, burned, or looted. Following the urban uprising, a fiercely anti-Asian sentiment continued to permeate sections of Los Angeles. In 1992–1993 there were a series of incidents of Asian Americans being harassed or beaten in southern California. After the rail-system contract was awarded to a Japanese company, a chauvinistic movement was launched to "buy American." Asian Americans are still popularly projected to other nonwhites as America's successful "model minorities," fostering resentment, misunderstandings, and hostilities among people of color. Yet black leaders have consistently failed to explain to the African Americans that Koreans, as a group, do not own the major corporations or banks that control access to capital. Asian Americans as a group do not own massive amounts of real estate, control the courts or city governments, have ownership in the mainstream media, dominate police forces, or set urban policies.

While African Americans, Latinos, and Asian Americans scramble over which group should control the mom-and-pop grocery store in their neighborhoods, almost no one questions the racist "redlining" policies of large banks that restrict access to capital to nearly all people of color. Black and Latino working people usually are not told by their race-conscious leaders and middle-class "symbolic representatives" that institutional racism has also frequently

targeted Asian Americans throughout U.S. history—from the recruitment and exploitation of Asian laborers, to a series of
lynchings and violent assaults culminating in the mass incarcera-
tion of Japanese Americans during World War II, to the slaying of
Vincent Chin in Detroit and the violence and harassment of other
Asian Americans.

A central ideological pillar of "whiteness" is the consistent
scapegoating of the "oriental menace." As legal scholar Mari Matsuda observes: "There is an unbroken line of poor and working
Americans turning their anger and frustration into hatred of Asian
Americans. Every time this happens, the real villains—the corporations and politicians who put profits before human needs—are
allowed to go about their business free from public scrutiny, and
the anger that could go to organizing for positive social change goes
instead to Asian-bashing."[5]

What is required is a radical break from the narrow, race-based
politics of the past, which characterized the core assumptions
about black empowerment since the mid-nineteenth century. We
need to recognize that both perspectives of racial identity politics,
which are frequently juxtaposed as integration/assimilation versus nationalist/separatism, are actually two different sides of the
same ideological axis. Racial identity politics must be challenged
in all communities of color in order to enhance the possibility of
coalitions.

The essential point of departure is the deconstruction of the idea
of "whiteness," the ideology of white power, privilege, and elitism
that remains heavily embedded within the dominant culture, social
institutions, and economic arrangements of the society. But we
must do more than critique the white pillars of race, gender, and
class domination and implicitly ask to join the status quo, by either
assimilating or "doing our own thing." We must rethink and re-
structure the central social categories of collective struggle by
which we conceive and understand our own political reality. We
must redefine "blackness" and other traditional racial categories to
be more inclusive of contemporary ethnic realities.

The factor of "race" by itself does not and cannot explain the
massive transformation of the structure of capitalism in its
postindustrial phase, and the destructive redefinition of work
itself as we enter the twenty-first century. Increasingly in western Europe and America, the new division of "haves" versus
"have-nots" is characterized by segmentation of the labor force.

The division is between those workers who have maintained basic economic security and benefits—such as full health insurance, term life insurance, pensions, educational stipends or subsidies for the employee's children, paid vacation, and so forth—versus those marginal workers who are either unemployed or part-time employees or who labor but have few, if any, benefits. Since 1982, "temporary employment" or part-time hirings without benefits have increased 250 percent across the United States, while all employment has grown by less than 20 percent. Today, the largest private employer in the United States is Manpower, Inc., the world's largest temporary employment agency, with 560,000 workers. By the year 2000, one-half of all American workers will be classified as part-time employees, or as they are termed within IBM, "the peripherals." The reason for this massive restructuring of labor relations is capital's search for surplus value or profits. In 1993, it is estimated that the total payroll costs in the United States of $2.6 billion annually will be reduced $800 million by the utilization of part-time laborers and employees.[6]

Increasingly, disproportionately high percentages of Latino and African American workers will be trapped within this second-tiered labor market. Black, Latino, Asian American, and low-income white workers all share a stake in fighting for a new social contract relating to work and social benefits. The right to a good job should be as firmly guaranteed as the human right to vote; the right to free quality health care should be as secure as the right to freedom of speech. The radical changes within the domestic economy require that black leadership reach out to other oppressed sectors of the society, creating a common program for economic and social justice.

A multicultural and democratic critique of U.S. politics must consider the changing demographic, cultural, and class realities of modern postindustrial America. By the year 2000, one-third of the total U.S. population will consist of people of color. Within seventy years, roughly one-half of America's entire population will be Latino, Native American, Asian American, Pacific American, Arab American, and African American. The ability to create a framework for multicultural democracy intergroup dialogue and interaction within and between the most progressive leaders, grassroots activists, intellectuals, and working people of these communities will determine the future of American society itself. Our ability to transcend racial chauvinism and interethnic hatred and the old definitions of "race," to recognize the class commonalities and joint social justice interests of all groups in the restructuring of this nation's economy and social order, will be the key in the construction of a nonracist democracy, transcending ancient walls of white violence, corporate power, and class privilege. By dismantling the narrow politics of racial identity and selective self-interest, by going beyond "black" and "white," we may construct new values, new institutions, and new visions of an America that can move beyond traditional racial categories and racial oppression.

NOTES

This chapter is based on an earlier version: "Beyond Racial Identity Politics: Towards a Liberation Theory for Multicultural Democracy" appearing in *Black America: The Street and the Campus* (London: Institute of Race Relations, 1993).

1. E. San Juan, "Racism, Ideology, Resistance," *Forward Motion*, vol. 10, no. 3 (September 1991), see pp. 35–42.

2. Cited in Manning Marable, "Beyond Racial Identity Politics: Towards a Liberation Theory for Multicultural Democracy," *Race and Class*, vol. 35, no. 1 (1993), p. 113.

3. For one point of view regarding the definition and description of Afrocentricity, see Molefi Asante, *The Afrocentric Idea* (Philadelphia: Temple University Press, 1988).

4. Cited in Marable, op. cit., p. 124.

5. Mari Matsuda, "Are Asian Americans a Racial Bourgeoisie?" *Katipunan*, vol. 4, no. 1 (September 1990), p. 12.

6. Marable, op. cit., p. 128.

Part II

Washington, D.C., Miami, and Los Angeles as Case Studies

4

Blacks and Latinos in the United States: The Emergence of a Common Agenda

Juanita Tamayo Lott

The population of people of color in the United States is growing at a high rate. In an increasing number of regions and localities, populations of African, Latino, Caribbean, and Asian Pacific origins have approached plurality status and even represent the overwhelming majority of the population in some places. This growth and distribution demands a new paradigm for describing and explaining the status and relationships of these population groups. Specifically, there is a greater need to understand communities of color not only in relationship to whites, but to each other. Issues affecting the diverse black and Latino populations of one city may differ vastly from the issues affecting these populations in other cities. The presence and composition of other people of color, such as Asians, and whites, also vary by locality and affect the dynamics within the locality. Policies and approaches that may be appropriate, for example, in San Francisco may be irrelevant in Washington, D.C., because of the difference in composition and organization of the Latino and black communities in terms of ethnicity, nativity, length of residence, socioeconomic status, political representation, and their proportion of the total population.

From a public policy perspective, the need to explore the political relations of these groups is extremely pressing during an economic stage characterized by large budget deficits at the local and national levels, scarce resources, and diminished governmental support for urban and local places. Often, blacks, Latinos, and Asians are forced to compete for insufficient and inadequate resources in education, health, social services, employment, economic development, and housing. Sadly (but perhaps, logically), this has sometimes resulted in intense group antagonisms. But, as pointed out in Chapter 1 by James Jennings, this situation may also provide opportunities for forging effective political coalitions.

The history of the Americas, as it involves people of color, provides a sociohistorical framework that should be noted and appreciated in discussions regarding coalitions between blacks and Latinos. The history of Latinos and blacks in the United States traditionally has been viewed outside of the mainstream of American history. Yet, blacks and Latinos settled in the Americas long before the "United States" even existed. The presence of black and Latino populations in the Americas can certainly be traced back to earlier than 1492. According to some accounts, Pedro Alonza Niño was a black sailor for Christopher Columbus's ship, the Santa María. Black explorers accompanied Spaniards such as Ponce de León, Cortéz, and Pizarro in their colonization of the New World. In 1538, Estevanico, a black explorer, led an expedition from Mexico into what is now the states of Arizona and New Mexico. Such events suggest that in some instances blacks and the European Hispanic ancestors had relationships as crew mates or members of expeditions. This information is not cited here, however, to diminish in any way the fact that the laws of Portugal and Spain permitted the subjugation of African peoples as slaves in their colonies. Rather, it is cited to suggest briefly some of the cultural linkages between these two groups of people.

A distinction between the colonization of North America and Spanish America (Mexico, Central, and South America) is that Anglo European colonizers included both men and women and sizable numbers of families who settled the New World while the Spaniards did not immigrate in such significant numbers to their colonies. The Spanish colonial population consisted mainly of men—explorers, missionaries, and soldiers—who intermarried with the "Indios" and blacks, creating a unique multicultural/multiracial population of Latinos. This is in contrast with the settlement of what is now the United States, where the new population was separated racially, with whites subjugating blacks. Blacks, both free and slave, were forced into a less-than-equal status.

This initial status as "less than equal" has shaped the history of blacks in the United States. The forced immigration of blacks to the United States began as early as 1619 when twenty black slaves arrived in Jamestown, Virginia. Almost two hundred years passed before the United States Congress banned the importation of black persons as slaves in 1808. For the first half of American history, blacks provided manual and skilled labor in the agricultural and industrial sectors of the South and North, not just as slaves but also as free persons of color. After emancipation, blacks began a migration north at first in few numbers and then in sizable numbers after World War I. They entered industrial and public-sector jobs, both civilian and military. Despite the emergence of a professional middle class, particularly since World War II, black workers have been concentrated in lower status and lower-paid positions in manufacturing and service industries.

Long before emancipation, blacks challenged their imposed status of less than equal. In doing so, they contributed to the democratization and political modernization of the United States by expanding the definition of American to include more than just whites. The *Negro Almanac* chronicles numerous slave revolts and acts of resistance to the status of "second class citizenship" that was imposed on black Americans.[1] Among the latter are included black soldiers fighting as early as 1747 for the English colony of South Carolina; free blacks establishing schools for the education of people of color in Philadelphia in 1818; publication of *Freedom's Journal*, the first black newspaper, published in 1827; and the formation of mutual aid societies before emancipation.

In the post–Civil War era, community-based religious, educational, and civic institutions were founded to support full citizenship of blacks. For example, Morehouse College in Atlanta and Howard University in Washington, D.C., were founded in 1867. The early twentieth century saw the establishment of two national black organizations, the National Association for the Advancement of Colored People (NAACP) founded in 1909 and the National Urban League in 1911. Most of the twentieth century witnessed the continuing struggle for equality by blacks, as individuals made their marks in all areas including the sciences, education, arts, humanities, law, and sports. Beginning with the New Deal, their contributions included landmark policies, most notably the development and enforcement of civil rights statutes and the creation of socioeconomic programs directed at the elimination of poverty.

As will be reiterated in the chapter by Daniel Osuna, the history of Latinos is both similar to and different from that of blacks. It is similar in that the presence of both groups in what is now the United States was forced on them. That is, African Americans were brought to America against their wills as slaves; Latinos were a conquered people in their own land. Since that initial contact of subjugation by whites, each population persistently has been treated as second-class citizens along with the indigenous peoples of the Americas and other people of color. There are, nevertheless, a few significant differences in the historical experiences of these groups.

Because they are English speaking and have resided in the United States since colonial times, blacks are more readily recognized as American citizens while Latinos are still perceived by many as foreigners because of their Spanish-speaking heritage and continuous immigration. With the tremendous increase of the Latino population in the 1970s and 1980s, coupled with the fact that many families maintain the use of the Spanish language in the home, there is an assumption that Latinos are new residents to the United States. Yet, most Latinos are native born.

With the signing of the Treaty of Guadalupe Hidalgo in 1848—in which a defeated Mexican government relinquished about half-a-million square miles of the Southwest to the United States—the history of Latinos as a major grouping within the postconquest United States began a new chapter. Well into the middle of the twentieth century, Mexican Americans comprised the largest subgroup of Latinos. With continued immigration of unskilled workers from Mexico, reinforced by American labor policies such as the Bracero Program, Mexican Americans continued to work in agricultural and other low-wage occupations. They continued to be concentrated in the Southwest for many generations.

Since 1917, Puerto Ricans have been American citizens, whether born in the Commonwealth or the mainland United States. On the other hand, in Florida and other parts of the country, Cubans represent a new sector of the U.S. Latino population. They came initially as refugees, beginning in the 1960s, but are increasingly becoming a native-born population as more second- and third-generation Cuban Americans are born and raised in the United States.

Due to various political and economic factors, efforts to improve the status of Mexican Americans became prominent during the mid-1960s.[2] In 1965, the United Farm Workers Union, composed of Mexican and Filipino grape workers, led a strike against grape growers of Delano, California, advocating for a minimum wage and improved working conditions. The strike was one spark contributing to the emergence of a Chicano Latino movement. Mexican Americans, joined by post–World War II communities of mainland Puerto Ricans and newly arrived Cuban immigrants throughout the 1970s and 1980s, advocated for equal opportunity policies in education, voting rights, employment, and language. They developed community-based and national organizations such as MALDEF (Mexican American Legal Defense and Education Fund) and the Southwest Voters Registration Education Project.

This history of political struggle is similar to that of blacks. While both groups initially were subjugated by whites—blacks as slaves and Latinos as a conquered people—both communities have continued to struggle throughout their history in the Americas for social equality. It is this particular historical fact that points to, and should encourage, the possibility of positive or cooperative, rather than negative or antagonistic, intergroup relations between these two groups in the urban United States today.

To some extent, cooperative relationships between blacks and Latinos were more evident in earlier years. Formal relationships between these communities of color were first noticeable during the social movements of the 1960s. With the civil rights movement highlighting the inequities experienced by blacks and other people of color and the antiwar movement depicting the disproportionate numbers of young black and Latino persons recruited to serve in the Vietnam War, people of color openly identified with each other in many instances and rallied around common concerns. It is important to note that these alliances were developed by these communities rather than by external sectors or actors. Early alliances were also found on campuses in schools of ethnic studies or Third World centers that included black studies, Chicano or Latino studies, Asian American stud-

Native American studies in their programs. The Black
r party developed a close working relationship with the
Pue.) Rican–based Young Lords party in places like New York
City and Chicago. As pointed out in the chapter by Jennings,
blacks and Puerto Ricans also have cooperated, at times, in the
arena of public education.

By the 1980s, several factors arose that challenged the capacity
and ability of blacks and various Latino groups to maintain and
expand earlier, cooperative intergroup relations. The most pressing
factor was the ability of these communities to maintain hard-won
civil rights and socioeconomic gains in the face of legal challenges
to affirmative-action policies and in a period of declining productivity. A second factor was the increasing diversity of national
origin within both of these groups due to expanded immigration.
This meant that even among themselves, blacks and Latinos, as
well as other groups of color, had to learn about and establish
relationships with people who were a part of these new populations and who may have spoken different languages and dialects
and come from different geographic and cultural backgrounds. A
third factor was the relatively rapid growth in these communities
within an urban political context of constricting economic productivity and opportunity.

A fourth factor was the emergence of a new generation of
black and Latino professionals who tended to reflect what Manning Marable refers to in his chapter as "symbolic representation." This factor tended to weaken the possibility of
political coalitions. First, as beneficiaries of affirmative action
policies, the new blacks and Latinos were trained, and worked,
in primarily "mainstream" institutions. These new professionals
were pioneers in traditionally white and male-dominated professions. Members identified on the basis of similar professions
formed associations that were occupationally specialized, and
not based on racial/ethnic communities. While people of color
with professional credentials historically have utilized their
skills within their own communities, the new generation of black
and Latino professionals was no longer limited to working in
their own communities. One effect of this development was that
the ability of a potential sector of leadership to represent or to
speak on behalf of its community was thus fragmented across
more and different professional subgroups and organizations.

This produced a weakening in the political potential of these communities, thereby diminishing the chance of developing strong political coalitions between these communities.

The 1990s began with a heightened sense of intergroup tensions and differences between communities of color. The national media has identified, and sensationalized, incidents of group antagonism among blacks, Latinos, and Asians. At the local level, sporadic efforts to improve relations among these groups exist but have yet to be systematically documented and analyzed. They range from ad hoc, individual actions for specific situations to planned initiatives by community organizations sometimes supported by a few foundations.

It should be noted that many community-initiated efforts often go unrecorded and unnoticed beyond the affected communities. Accounts intermittently appear in the media or in foundation-based project reports. While the federal government provided some initial, external impetus for black and Latino communities to dialogue and work together in recent years, some in corporate philanthropy have also sought to bring these groups together. This is a particularly important development because it suggests that harmonious relations between communities of color does influence the broader business environment. Various foundations have initiated pilot projects in selected communities nationwide that focus on and require diverse neighborhood coalitions.

While these external efforts should be applauded and expanded, it must also be appreciated that the policy agendas for black and Latino communities have been established over several decades and need not be reinvented. They have as their basic premise—as is suggested in the history of both blacks and Latinos—the achievement of social justice, equal opportunity, and access and representation at local, state, and national political levels. For the most part, although they may appear as group-specific policies, these policy agendas are directed to structural changes in institutions controlling the quality and distribution of education, health care, employment, income, and housing for broad groups of people.

Blacks and Latinos face three major issues that together represent a potential unifying policy agenda. One basic issue that could serve to unite the political agendas of black and Latino populations is the well-being of their communities and families. Given the socioeconomic profile of blacks and Latinos, the survival of some segments of their communities and the survival of each group as a unique people have become issues of continuing debate. While kinship bonds and shared heritage, including spiritual values, have been the primary basis of group unity and identity, the black and Latino populations are being challenged by rapidly deteriorating socioeconomic status.

Immigration, despite its potential for divisiveness, can also be a unifying theme. Much of the tension and competition among different populations is due to an assumption that entitlement to goods and services is related to citizenship and length of residence in the United States. With the growth of a transnational and multiracial/multicultural labor force around the world, the idea of citizenship may become far less important due to global economic pressures. Indeed, new and critical policy-related questions for viable intergroup relations are: What are the unique rights and responsibilities of American citizens that are distinguishable from those of noncitizens? Are there appropriate rights and responsibilities for immigrants and language minorities? And, more specifically, what is the impact of recent black immigrants on the black community? Concomitantly, what is the impact of new Latino immigrants on the Latino community? What is the impact of immigrants who, increasingly, are neither black nor Hispanic? These are questions that both groups must grapple with; but the answers must be such that political collaboration, rather than conflict, is the result. Both groups gain benefits from collaboration, and both will lose if conflict alone is the result.

In the past, the United States has been viewed as a land of opportunity and upward mobility by both native residents and immigrants. This view is now open to question with continuing disparities between whites and people of color. Even with increased labor force participation, black and Latino men and women have lower incomes than the general population. One out of three black persons is poor; one out of four persons of Latin origin is poor. While middle-class status for all families is increasingly dependent on two wage earners, for some lower-income families, including Latinos and blacks, earned income has been replaced by welfare income. This stagnation in economic mobility is hurting blacks and Latinos in peculiar ways. Yet, economic mobility can be a third unifying theme. Relevant policy questions regarding economic mobility and political empowerment are: In what ways can power (such as ownership or control of land, capital, marketable skills) be created and/or increased for established and emerging Latino and black communities? What are viable roles for these young populations, as they constitute a critical mass of the labor force? Who can produce and/or negotiate power on behalf of these communities? These questions can be answered in ways that are not divisive, yet acknowledge the historical and continuing struggle for social justice and equality that is reflected in the experiences of these communities.

The Latino and black populations are growing and becoming larger segments of the American population. They have historically occupied lower socioeconomic status. Furthermore, both populations contain a substantial proportion of America's youth, including vast numbers who are being raised in poverty. The continued survival of the United States is dependent upon the well-being of these residents.

Recognition of these different groups is just beginning, as is a deeper understanding. Efforts to promote intra- and intergroup relations are under way even as intergroup tensions escalate. Despite local nuances regarding relations between communities of color, it is clear that during the 1990s a dialogue between established and emerging black and Latino communities within a multicultural, multiracial, and global policy perspective can be significant and pioneering. Such dialogue can lead to a new stage of intergroup relations that will help continue the democratization of the United States and, perhaps, thereby take our nation to a new stage of economic health and stability.

NOTES

This chapter is excerpted from "Towards a Greater Understanding of Black and Hispanic Relations: Demographic, Historical and Policy Perspectives," a monograph commissioned by the Community Relations Service, U.S. Department of Justice, October 1990.

1. See Harry Ploski and James Williams, eds., *The Negro Almanac: A Reference Work on the Afro-American*, 4th ed. (New York: Wiley, 1983).

2. In earlier decades, Latino organizations actively involved in the struggle for equal rights included the League of United Latin

American Citizens (LULAC) founded in the 1920s and the G.I.
Forum composed of World War II veterans.

5

The State and Future of Black/Latino Relations in Washington, D.C.: A Bridge in Need of Repair

Keith Jennings and Clarence Lusane

Perhaps one of the most troubling aspects of the contemporary civil rights and equal rights movements is the apparent growing animus between national minority groups. The tension between the two largest national groups of color in the United States, African Americans and Latinos, has been evident in a number of major jurisdictions across the country. In Houston, Chicago, and Miami, different approaches to the issue of reapportionment exacerbate existing political divisions and, in part, are exploited by the white power structure. In other locations, such as Los Angeles and New York, long-standing brown-black alliances are being torn apart by the local reverberations of the devastating national economic crisis, the competitive fight for jobs, and differing access to political power.

At the same time, a number of developments provide evidence that unity between these two groups is desired and being sought. The recent death of Cesar Chavez, one of the most respected Latino leaders known to many in the African American community, brought out a number of national black leaders to recall his legacy. The NAACP (National Association for the Advancement of Colored People), under the leadership of Ben Chavis, announced the aggressive opening of the organization to Latinos (although there were never formal restrictions before), signaling that civil rights is not just a black issue and that some black leaders are determined to reach out across the nation to other minorities.

Both blacks and Latinos have a common interest in combating racism whose various forms often impact differently, but, in the final analysis, with equal denial of human and civil rights. As the United States heads into the twenty-first century, these contradicting tendencies of conflict and coalition provide a timely interlude to assess the nature of the relationship between the two communities and to consider what is driving that relationship, either positively or negatively.

This chapter investigates the state of black-Latino relations in Washington, D.C., and analyzes the sources of the tensions and possibilities for unity between the communities. While the problem of the conflicts between the two communities is often alluded to, no consensus exists on what has caused those differences. The current state of relations between blacks and Latinos, to a great degree, has been shaped by class and political factors that have been out of the control of those two communities. At both national and local levels, cold war politics during the period of Reaganism, changes in the political economy of urban America, and the nature of modern black electoral politics have combined to create an interethnic tension that dominates much of what constitutes black and Latino relations today.

The increase in Latino residents in a number of cities, including Washington, D.C., was partially driven by the Reagan administration's sponsorship and coordination of region-wide conflicts in Central America. From Nicaragua and Honduras to Guatemala and El Salvador, Central American refugees streamed into the United States to escape war-ravaged villages and towns beset by armies that were truly "made in the U.S.A." Most, if not the overwhelming majority, of those uprooted peasants and workers, many of whom did not speak English, came to the cities and almost immediately melded into the underclass of the unemployed and underemployed.

The departure of manufacturing firms from urban areas in the United States, coupled with staggering decreases in federal aid, threw countless cities into an economic quagmire of catastrophic proportions that strained city services and wrecked city budgets. These cuts were driven by the suburbanization of America, which reflected itself in antiurban federal policies from both the Republican-controlled White House and the Democratic-controlled

Congress. The "white flight" and even "black flight" of middle-class residents further weakened the capacity of urban leaders to address the needs of their poorest residents who remain disproportionately Latino and black. Thus, not only did black and Latino urban residents become poorer, they also became more numerous as a proportion of the city's population.

This new urban picture was unfolding as African Americans began to assume management and political leadership responsibilities for a number of big cities including Philadelphia, Chicago, and New York among others. In a few cities with significant Latino populations, such as Los Angeles, black mayors have strengthened their political base and positions based on the understanding that they would deliver first and foremost to the black community. These cities, however, have experienced a large influx of undocumented Latino immigrants who vie for depleted economic resources along with working class and impoverished African Americans.

Washington, D.C., is no exception to this kind of political situation. In addition, however, the District of Columbia's "colonial" relationship to the federal government qualitatively impacts on the city's capacity to address issues of inequality that disproportionately affect both its Latino and black communities. Denied the ability to make its own laws, unable to determine how and who it taxes, and limited by a lack of full representation in Congress, D.C.'s powerlessness to guide its own affairs has been central to exacerbating the polarization among various social, racial, and ethnic groups in the city; this is a key point in this chapter.

It must be pointed out that efforts to overcome ethnic tensions between blacks and Latinos have been ongoing in the city. In particular, attempts to bridge the cultural divide between the two groups, often the most immediate and personal source of discord, have been made by both black and Latino activists. For the most part, these efforts have been made by progressives and leftists rather than by the city's established or elected black or Latino leaders.

The African American population in the nation's capital between 1970 and 1990 has changed significantly. Some of these changes have influenced the nature of political relations between blacks and Latinos. Before the desegregation victories of the mid-1960s, as in a number of other cities across the country, there was a solid black community with businesspersons, professionals, and working-class families living together. However, as a result of the gains of the civil rights and black power movements, class stratification allowed some African Americans to move into areas formerly restricted because of residential segregation. Washington's black urban rebellion of 1968, following the assassination of Martin Luther King, Jr., led to the destruction of the 14th and H streets black business and commercial strips that, at that time, were booming. In the wake of the rebellion few small black businesses were rebuilt, and today Koreans, Africans, and Caribbean islanders have replaced African Americans as shop owners in the black community.

The small Latino population that lived in Washington, D.C., prior to the civil wars in Central America was a racially mixed, relatively educated group from across Latin America. Although language barriers existed, most found work, although jobs and income varied widely depending on skill and education level. However, as pointed out above, Washington, D.C., became an important relocation destination for large numbers of often undocumented Central American refugees as a result of the intensification of the civil wars in the 1980s. Most of the recent Latino immigrants to the city are from rural backgrounds, largely uneducated, and overwhelmingly from Central America. Most are also more identifiable as people of color.

At the beginning of the 1990s, the District's population was estimated to be 65 percent black, 28 percent white, between 5 and 12 percent Latino, and 2 percent Asian.[1] The total Latino population in the District, as indicated by the above statistics, is a source of dispute with many Latino leaders believing that a serious undercount exists. The official District government figures place the Latino population at 32,710 making it 4 to 5 percent of the city's population.[2] Table 5.1, based on data from the U.S. Bureau of the Census, shows how this population is divided among various Latino groups.

Table 5.1
Latino Population Groups in Washington, D.C.

Mexican American	2,981
Puerto Rican	2,204
Cuban	1,241
Other Hispanic	26,284
Total Population (all persons)	32,710

The Office of Latino Affairs uses the figure of 65,000 as the total Latino population, making the proportion about 10 percent of the total D.C. population. The Latino Civil Rights Task Force, another Latino community group, has argued that the Latino population for the city is 85,000, thus making the Latino population 12 percent of the District's total.

Some efforts were made by city officials to address the needs of the growing Latino population. These steps were inadequate, however, and as a result, Latinos rebelled in 1991 in the Mount Pleasant section of the city (discussed in detail below). This crisis led to the public airing of grievances felt by both communities toward each other. Many Latinos felt that their community's concerns had been neglected by the city's ruling black elite, and many African Americans felt that Latinos did not respect the history of blacks in producing some social change beneficial to all groups. The crisis also led to the first serious efforts to assess the role and status of Latinos in Washington, D.C., and to proposals for improving the relations between communities as well as addressing issues specific to Latinos.

President Ronald Reagan's wars against communism in Central America triggered an exodus of Latino immigrants of major proportions. Arguing that communism had to be stopped at the U.S. border, Reagan's not-so-secret and bloody covert operations against the Sandinistas in Nicaragua and the antigovernment forces in El Salvador drove thousands of displaced and war-weary peasants and workers to enter the United States and take up undocumented residences in cities like Los Angeles, San Francisco, and Washington, D.C.[3] As a result, the greatest proportion of Latinos in the District now come from El Salvador. Mexican Americans, Puerto Ricans, and Cubans, the largest Latino populations nationally, are only about 20 percent of the District's Latino population as indicated in Table 5.1. In addition, a sizable Latino population from Nicaragua, the Dominican Republic, Panama, and Guatemala is also present. Whereas the earlier generation of Latinos in the Washington area had come from countries in South America and tended to be white and middle to upper class, the new immigrants were overwhelmingly poor and clearly of darker color. The factor of geographical origin for the immigrant Latino population in Washington, D.C., is a very important consideration with respect to perceptions and attitudes regarding issues such as racism and discrimination as we discuss below.

Overall, Latinos and Asians became among the fastest growing ethnic minorities in the metropolitan Washington, D.C., area. During the period 1980–1990, they grew by 85 percent and 69 percent, respectively.[4] It is not, therefore, surprising that African Americans and Latinos live side by side in a number of areas throughout the District. Some studies have indicated, as a matter of fact, that dark-skinned or black Latinos tend to move into African American neighborhoods while light-skinned or Anglo Latinos tend to move closer to white areas. The pattern described above is generally true of the nation's capital as well. For instance, one reason why more Latinos live in the predominantly white Ward 3 section of the city than African Americans is that many white Latinos, in the earlier periods, settled there rather than in parts of the city that were more overwhelmingly African American.

Class issues also come into play in housing because most Latinos in the city are poor and live in overcrowded dwellings. A number of community activists speculate that such conditions exist because Latinos have been used as temporary wedges for taking over poor black communities only to eventually be cast aside themselves for gentrification. This is what occurred in the culturally chic and now racially diverse areas of Adams Morgan and Mount Pleasant. In 1980, blacks were as much as 70 percent of the population in those communities. Today, African Americans constitute only 40 percent of the residents in those neighborhoods. These areas were long ago targeted by commercial developers and real estate barons to be the "next Georgetown" feasting off the disposable income of "yuppies."

Afro-Latinos constitute approximately 13 percent of the total Latino population in Washington, D.C., and live mostly in racially mixed Ward 1.[5] Afro-Latinos represent a potential bridge between the two communities that is often ignored by both blacks and Latinos. While rapid and diverse Latino population growth occurred, as described above, the African American population declined from 448,906 to 399,604, a full 11 percent over the same period.[6]

THE URBAN CRISIS IN BLACK AND BROWN

Black and Latino relations must be carefully placed within a framework that appreciates the magnitude of the urban crisis and the way it expresses itself in racial and ethnic terms. African

Americans and Latinos are the most urbanized national minority groups in the United States. The much-discussed and reality-based crisis of the cities disproportionately affects these groups more than any other U.S. racial or ethnic communities. The overall fiscal crisis, budget cuts, and the general abandonment of the central cities by the private sector and the federal government have led to intensified squabbles among city occupants for fair dispensation of scarce resources and services. By one estimate, "the 64 percent cutback in federal aid since 1980 had cost cities $26 billion per year (in constant 1990 dollars). For cities with more than 300,000 inhabitants, the average federal share of the municipal income stream has plummeted from 22 percent in 1980 to a mere 6 percent in 1989."[7] This has meant, for example, that in New York, federal aid as a percent of the city's budget dropped from 19 percent in 1977 to 9 percent in 1985.[8] In Los Angeles, the drop was from 18 percent to 2 percent; in Chicago from 27 percent to 15 percent; in Detroit from 23 percent to 12 percent; and in Baltimore from 20 percent to 6 percent.[9]

For Washington, D.C., the combination of recession and federal payment reductions led to severe strains on an already economically depressed city. In 1990, about 50 percent of all District households had annual earnings below $20,000 and 20 percent had household incomes below $10,000.[10] In addition, more than 30 percent of the residents in the District "received financial assistance from supplemental assistance programs such as Medicaid, food stamps, or Aid to Families with Dependent Children."[11]

In short, this has meant that the District, similar to most major urban cities, had to provide social services, educational opportunities, and jobs to an increasingly poor, unemployed, and diverse population—all while the options to raise revenue constricted. Already in the position of imposing one of the highest tax burdens on residents of any jurisdiction in the United States, District officials were well aware that even discussion of a tax increase would lead to greater middle-class revolt. The decrease in the city's population suggests that those residents who could afford to move out did. In the 1980s, as in many other parts of the country, those who left the city were mostly from east of the

Potomac River in the black and disproportionately poor Wards 5, 6, 7, and 8.

The contrast between city residents, with wealth and influence concentrated in the mainly white Ward 3 and poverty, misery, and unemployment concentrated in the almost all black seventh and eighth wards, is one indication of the complex matrix of race, ethnicity, and prejudice in Washington, D.C., and most other urban settings today, regardless of who the managers are downtown. Ward 3, for example, has a median household income of $48,967. In Ward 8, which has the highest proportion of African Americans, the median income level is $21,312. More than 20 percent of the residents in Wards 5, 7, and 8 live below the poverty line while, not surprisingly, those wards can also boast the highest unemployment rates in the city.[12]

In the area of employment it is significant to note that Latinos were employed during the boom period of the 1980s at a rate higher than African Americans in the construction industry in the District and that they quickly moved into the service industries. These were the main growth sectors of the District's economy. In a number of areas—including office maintenance, hotel, and restaurant work—Latinos were able to find steady work. Thus a good percentage of the new Latino entrants into the workforce were absorbed until the recession of 1989. These positions were low-paying jobs such as laborers, waiters, and dishwashers.

Yet, a perception exists in the African American community that Latinos have taken jobs formerly reserved for them in the District's segmented labor market.[13] Many of the city's restaurant, hotel, and janitorial jobs traditionally employed blacks as cooks, waiters, janitors, and doormen. Recently, however, Latinos have begun to fill these job slots in record numbers, leading many blacks to contend that "the Latinos are taking over."

Two reasons are advanced as to why young black males do not pursue or obtain these jobs. One is that many young, un-skilled, and uneducated black males feel that these jobs are beneath them and that there is more money to be made by engaging in illegal activities, primarily drug trafficking. A sec-ond view is offered by writer Andrew Hacker who argues that whites prefer to employ Latinos because they feel uncomfortable around blacks. Hacker states, "White employers can sense racial tensions, and often seek to avoid them by hiring more acquies-cent Filipinos or Hispanics. . . . Sad to say, many white Americans feel uncomfortable in establishments that have a pronounced number of black employees."[14]

Interestingly, however, Latino employment with the District government is equally dismal. Although Latinos are at least 5 percent of the District's population, and perhaps twice that amount, they represented only 1 percent of the city's workers. In 1992, out of roughly 31,400 employees of the District government's various agencies and departments, only 529 were Latino. Of the 19,723 employees of city agencies independent of the mayor's office, about 216 were Latino.[15] As late as 1990, only 1.6 percent of the District government's employees were Latino. In addition, only 4 of the District's city council's 172 employees were Latino. When considered with the fact that about 11 percent of the city's residents are employed by the District government, on the surface, a good case for hiring discrimination exists. It was against this social and economic backdrop that the city confronted its most violent social disturbance in a generation: the Mount Pleasant uprising.

MOUNT PLEASANT REBELLION

On May 5, 1991, the police shooting of Daniel Enrique Gomez during a Cinco de Mayo celebration in the Mount Pleasant area of the city became the catalyst for three days and nights of street battles between Latino (and black) youths and the District police. The incident and the battles that followed became a watershed moment in the role of Latinos in the city. As activist and attorney Luis Rumbaut stated, "From now on, Latinos will be seen as a critical part of the city's population."[16]

The police, long viewed as an occupying army by many of the city's Latinos, claimed that Gomez attempted to stab one of the officers, a rookie, who tried to arrest him for being drunk and disorderly. Latino community residents contended that Gomez was fully handcuffed and had no weapon. As word spread about the shooting, Latino youth began to vent against not only the Gomez shooting, but patterns of systematic police harassment and frustration with the city's benign neglect concerning Latino issues. Tensions within the community were already high as many middle-class white, and not a few black, residents repeatedly demanded police intervention to stop public urination, drunkenness, and loitering from the many unemployed Latino men who hung out on street corners in the neighborhood.

The situation worsened when Latino community leaders felt insulted that Mayor Sharon Pratt Kelly, in office only five months, did not come initially to the community to try to restore calm and failed to show at a meeting of Latino community leaders the morning after the first night of riots. On the second night of disturbance, Latino youth were joined by, and in some estimates outnumbered by black youths. Stores were looted, buildings burned, and a running, rock-throwing battle with the police lasted for much of the night. By the third day, with a massive show of over 1,000 police, a relative peace had returned to the area and the mayor and other city officials were calling desperate meetings with Latino leaders. While some black city leaders publicly called for unity, others launched verbal attacks on Latinos. Popular black radio host Cathy Hughes, for example, stated that the mayor should "round them up, herd them up, check their green cards, turn them over to immigration, and get them out of my neighborhood, out of my city."[17]

Most Latino leaders referred to the Mount Pleasant events as a "race riot." Was the May 1991 Mount Pleasant rebellion a race riot of Latinos against blacks and whites, a class riot of the area's poor against the petty bourgeois managers of the state, or a youth riot of unbridled frustration against police harassment? To some degree, it was all of these phenomena. Arguments can certainly be made that a racial character was evident. Gomez was shot by a black police officer, the fact of which helped to fuel the suspicion that he was shot because he was Hispanic. At the same time, evidence exists that suggests a class anger drove the uprising to some degree. Many of those who participated in the riot, according to press interviews, saw the looting and burning as attacks on power and privilege. The uprising became their means of striking back at a system that paid them little attention. Only a short time earlier, many Latinos in the Washington area, particularly Salvadorans, had lost their life savings when the uninsured Latino Investment Corporation went under. City officials responsible for overseeing the operations of financial institutions in the city had ignored the questionable behavior of the bank's owner until it was too late.

Latino community relations with the city's police were probably at an all-time low. Latino and black youths, in particular, had often complained about police harassment and mistreatment. At the time of the riot, the city had a backlog of more than 700 police brutality cases. Most of those cases, however, were not submitted by Latino residents. Language barriers and fear of exposure of illegal status meant that Latinos did not express their ire through official means. Young Hispanic men did informally complain to various Latino social agencies about being harassed. Black youths also felt that police unnecessarily harassed them at youth dance clubs and other youth gatherings. Attacks on the police were a unifying theme for Latinos and blacks. Over one-half of all persons arrested during the rebellion were young African Americans.

Most observers and official reports argued that the primary cause of the rebellion was the frustration of "a growing Hispanic population whose needs are being underserved by government, but it is also a reflection of a more general national problem of mounting racial and ethnic tensions."[18] As noted above, this was not exactly the case, and the three-day rebellion could not be explained in conventional race-relations terms nor could its complexity be understood without a clear appreciation for the quasi-colonial context in which the black elite exercises power in the District of Columbia.

BLACK EMPOWERMENT: BROWN OPPRESSION

Rapid growth in the District's Latino population caught black city officials by surprise and found them unprepared, politically and administratively, to address that community's concerns and issues. Despite the city having been majority African American since the 1950s, it had been less than two decades since the city's black leaders had come to power. Under pressure from civil rights activists, residents won the right to vote for the president in 1963, for school board in 1968, for a nonvoting delegate to Congress in 1971, and for mayor and city council three years later. In 1974, the city elected its first primarily black city council and black mayor, Walter Washington. However, it wasn't until the 1978 election of the reformist administration of Marion Barry, a former nationalist civil rights leader, that African Americans in the city truly began to gain administrative power. In his first term as mayor, Barry hired thousands of blacks into city government, doled out millions in minority contracts, and established community programs that benefited poor and working-class residents of the city. His social service programs for seniors and a summer jobs program for the city's youth endeared him to the black community even as the fiscal contradictions of those programs began to break the city's economic mold.

As valuable as those initiatives were, they did not address the structural limits of the city's political and economic system. At the same time problems affecting the poor in the city continued to mount. By the time Barry left office in 1990, the fiscal crisis of the city was entrenched and about to usher in an era of government cuts in workers and social services and little hope of turning the situation around.

It was in this context that the city's black leaders came face-to-face with the new social ripples brought by a growing and demanding Latino population. Black city leaders, under electoral pressure to deliver to those who got them in office, found little political value in calling for expanded services to Latinos in an atmosphere of shrinking resources. For example, the city's educational system had to immediately address the concerns of language minorities while social service delivery mechanisms had to create desperately needed bilingual materials. In both of these areas, the city was woefully lacking.

What also began to loom as a critical concern was the issue of political representation. Latinos represent less than 1 percent of the total registered voters in the District. This lack of voting power has meant that virtually no Latinos have been in an official position to bring about change. Since 1968, when the city first won the ability to elect a school board and later a city council, there has been only one elected Latino, Frank Schaffer-Corona, who had been a controversial and radical member of the school board until his defeat in 1981. Though he represented the Latino community in often militant ways and challenged conservative drifts by the city's leadership, his confrontational style and frequently politically eccentric behavior isolated and prevented him from building the type of coalitions needed to advance a progressive agenda. During the Iranian hostage crisis, for example, he used school board phones to call Iran and try to negotiate a resolution to the crisis. In 1987, he was indicted on embezzlement charges when he was accused by a local D.C. bank of misusing $25,000 that was accidentally deposited into a bank account of his.[19] He was eventually captured in Texas, sent back to the District where he was found guilty, and sentenced to prison.

Even among the city's numerous advisory neighborhood commissioners Latinos are vastly underrepresented. The commissioners are elected representatives of small neighborhood divisions that address issues affecting the local community. As of May 1992, of the 323 elected advisory neighborhood commissioners, only one was Latino.[20]

Important administrative attempts to address Latino issues occurred during the Barry years. Attempting to define and meet the needs of the city's Latinos and pressed by Latino activists, Barry created the Office of Latino Affairs and the Commission on Latino Business Development. The Office of Latino Affairs (OLA) was set up to be an advocacy group within the District government. The Commission on Latino Community Development was developed to advise the mayor and the council on the needs and views of the Latino community. The Commission consists of fifteen voting members appointed by the mayor and subject to council approval and eight ex-officio nonvoting members. The Commission has a statutory responsibility of developing a list of three names from which the mayor must choose the directors of OLA.

The relationship between the OLA and the Commission was one of the most controversial issues prior to the Mount Pleasant rebellion. Once Sharon Pratt Kelly won the mayoral race over Marion Barry in 1990, a general attitude arose in the incoming mayor's administration that everything Barry had done should either be discarded, dismantled, or held in suspicion. Thus, when the Barry-appointed Latino Commission made the three required recommendations for Director of the OLA, Kelly refused to appoint any one of the nominated candidates, stating that she would wait until a "suitable" candidate was suggested. Kelly eventually did appoint Maria Lopez as acting director and on April 30, 1992, more than a year after she entered office, Kelly named Carmen Ramirez as permanent OLA director. The fact that the OLA had no permanent leadership and the Commission itself was forced to resign exacerbated the wide division between the Latino leadership and the new Kelly administration. It also did not help the situation that the only two Latinos in Kelly's cabinet were from outside the District.

THE LATINO TASK FORCE AND THE U.S. CIVIL RIGHTS COMMISSION REPORT

One group developing out of the Mount Pleasant situation was the D.C. Latino Civil Rights Task Force. Comprised of representatives from a cross section of the Latino community, the task force had spurned Kelly's initial invitation to become tied to her administration and decided to play the role of an outside advocacy organization. In its initial stage of development, the task force attempted to represent all of the diverse segments of the Latino community and thereby become a united front capable of addressing in a new way a Latino agenda for the city. The task force maintained a close working relationship with established Latino civil rights organizations based in the city as well as with the National Council on La Raza also based in Washington. One of its first demands was a call for an investigation by the U.S. Civil Rights Commission on whether the civil rights of Latinos in the city had been violated.

At the same time, Afro-Latinos within the task force sought to have the question of racism within the Latino community addressed. Controversy arose about this issue, however, and consequently many of the Puerto Rican, Panamanian, and Dominican activists disassociated themselves from the task force and its agenda.

In January 1993, the release of the much-anticipated U.S. Civil Rights Commission report entitled, "Race and Ethnic Tensions in American Communities: Poverty, Inequality and Discrimination, Volume 1: The Mount Pleasant Report," generated another spike in the relations between the city government and the Latino community. The report was the first in what is to be a series of Commission reviews on racial and ethnic tensions across the nation. The Commission chair at that time, moderate black Republican Arthur Fletcher, stated the following rationale for and significance of the report:

Although the focus of this report is on civil rights issues affecting the Latino community in Washington, D.C. our findings and recommendations, particularly with respect to police misconduct and the lack of bilingual services in critical areas such as health, social services, education and criminal justice, will likely apply to other localities across the nation.[21]

The Commission responded to this change by selecting the District as the project's first hearing site and immediately began a six-month investigation of the Latino task force's allegations which included: violations of civil rights of Latinos, police abuse of Latino residents, discriminatory hiring practices by the D.C. government, and system-wide failure by the District to provide social services to the Latino community.

The 173–page report covers eight specific areas and provides a general overview of Latinos in the District as well as the immigration situation confronting many Salvadoran refugees. The eight areas covered include the following: (1) police-community relations; (2) civilian oversight of policing; (3) Latinos in the District Court System; (4) Equal Employment Opportunity in District government; (5) Latino access to social services; (6) Latino access to health care; (7) low-income housing; and (8) educational opportunity. The findings of the Commission are harsh in several areas. For example, in the area of housing the report finds,

The District has a host of affordable housing programs, but lacks an effective comprehensive affordable housing strategy to deal with these problems. Latinos suffer, in particular, from the District's failure to enforce its housing code effectively and sensitively, sometimes with the result that Latino and other residents are evicted from their homes because the District has failed to force landlords to maintain their buildings up to code.[22]

In the area of equal employment opportunity, the Commission found,

The agency heads generally have not through their own initiative recruited a sufficient number of bilingual personnel in positions having public contact with Spanish speaking clientele, despite the obvious need. . . . The Hispanic Employment Program has not been allocated any funds for recruitment, and the individual agencies do not submit to the Hispanic program officer any reports regarding recruitment or employment statistics.[23]

And in the area of police-community relations, the Commission found,

The Third District [Police Station], which has the highest concentration of Latinos, had the highest overall Civilian Complaint Review Board CCRB complaint rate during the 1985–1991 period; the highest complaint rate from residents; the most multiple complaint officers . . . and the highest number of disorderly conduct arrests over a 5–year period. Yet, the Third District did not have the highest crime rate or the highest number of service calls or officers assigned per capita, factors that might account for the high complaint rate.[24]

The Commission report was criticized from a number of quarters. The District government, including the mayor's office and the police department, felt that the report was unbalanced and failed to address the progress that had been made by the city in providing services to the Latino community. Many activists also criticized the report. Some felt that methodological flaws as well as a political myopia regarding the true nature of the District's problems dominated the report. Input was limited, many felt, to government officials and a few selected Latino leaders. Key actors who had been in the forefront of attempting to bridge positive relations between the Latino and black communities were not questioned or were denied input.

Some activists also believed that another major flaw was the Commission's view that the lack of statehood had only a minor impact on the capabilities of the city to manage its affairs. The authors of the report seem to be convinced that the District's problems can be solved without first addressing the quasi-colonial relationship between the District and the federal government. A recurring and growing cry of the civil rights movement has focused on the lack of statehood for the District of Columbia. Under the current status, the federal government can and does intervene in local affairs on a regular basis.

The city was created and is ruled by the federal government. Unlike residents in every other state in the nation, the District's citizens, even today, do not have full representation in Congress, control over their budget, the power to tax, or the ability to make and finalize their own laws. Control of the city's budget by the federal government, when coupled with the general fiscal crisis, has led to severe cutbacks in many social programs. Commenting on this reality, a special commission on budget and financial priorities set up in 1991 to develop a fiscal strategy for the District concluded that the federal government had not contributed its fair share to the District's budget and that it should either eliminate certain restrictions on the District's taxing power or increase the federal payment.[25] By the late 1980s, the District found itself in a position of having to make cutbacks in personnel and city services at a time when the need was growing rapidly. While this austerity meant cutbacks for the city's black poor, for Latinos it also meant that many programs and services would never get implemented.

THE FUTURE OF BLACK-LATINO RELATIONS IN THE NATION'S CAPITAL

Although there are strong pressures, internal and external, pushing a continual deterioration in black and Latino relations, countervailing winds are blowing. A number of activists and groups have dedicated themselves to building strong and lasting ties between the two communities. One group that has been in the forefront of the efforts to bring together the two communities is the Coalition for African American and Latino Unity (CAALU). Begun in 1990, CAALU has as its goals "to improve the relationship between African American and Latino individuals and organizations by promoting better understanding, mutual respect, cooperation, and harmony; to support the efforts and encourage the development of local community-based organizations working for basic rights and community empowerment and against discrimination; and to forge links and exchange information with local, national, and international groups with similar goals."[26] The politically progressive CAALU is made up of black and Latino groups and individuals who have sponsored political forums and cultural programs to bridge the gap between these groups in the city. CAALU members have also represented the two communities at international conferences and meetings where issues of multiculturalism have been discussed.

Another organization to evolve out of the Mount Pleasant incident was the D.C. Community Coalition. It was chaired by local civil rights leader Maudine Cooper and Tony Montes, a staff aide to D.C. Delegate Eleanor Holmes Norton. Representatives of the city's black and brown elite initiated the group in an effort to get out in front on the issue of multiracial unity in the city. Among the groups who joined the Community Coalition were the NAACP, the Urban League, the D.C. Latino Civil Rights Task Force, CAALU, the United Planning Organization, and numerous black and Latino social service agencies and organizations. The group would eventually fade, but one of its main contributions to healing the divisions in the city was its sponsorship of the January 1992 Citywide Multicultural Leadership Summit.

Addressing ethnic and racial tensions in the District has meant the inevitable development of efforts concerned with the high levels of poverty, unemployment, and homelessness among blacks and Latinos. The summit was one of the most successful efforts preceding from this perspective in the wake of the riots. The purpose of the summit was to gather activists, leaders, and concerned citizens to address the complex challenges facing the District as it evolves into a multiracial urban center. The goal, as envisioned by the organizers, "was to bring together community leaders from all over the city to talk about common problems and to develop a series of recommendations that will foster and preserve the 'tapestry' that is this city."[27]

More than 500 people attended the Summit's reception, plenaries, and workshops with representation of Native Americans, Chinese, Koreans, Indochinese, Hispanics, West Indians, African Americans, Africans, and whites. Religious diversity was also present with participation from the Baptist, Protestant, Jewish, Islamic, Catholic, and other faiths. Participation from city leaders and elected officials, including city council, school board, and advisory neighborhood commission members, was also high. D.C. Shadow Senator Jesse Jackson gave one of the keynote speeches for the summit. Jackson argued that it was important that people have a sense of culture and history in order to advance into the future and in order to empower themselves. He concluded his remarks by stating to those in attendance that "your presence represents mind expansion and cultural growth."[28]

The organizers believed that the summit was successful, although some activists complained that the organizers of the event did not collaborate with the leaders of the community coalition as much as they should. Those involved with the project felt that it could serve as a model for future efforts aimed at discovering the underlying reasons behind ethnic and racial conflict. According to Arturo Griffiths, the principal event organizer, it became clear to most participants that the ethnic and racial conflict in the city and nation has deep and complex roots, many resulting from the intersection of different political and social factors.[29]

The efforts of these groups are commendable and reflect a genuine desire for united efforts in addressing common concerns and mutual interests. At the same time, these groups and other groups who attempt to end the animosities and conflicts between the Latino and black communities must build a bridge that can theoretically and politically carry the weight of this complicated relationship. Class issues, in particular, confront both of these communities internally and externally. A black and brown elite have often demonstrated opportunism that has undermined the efforts at unity around issues that disproportionately affect the poor and working class components of these communities. The disdain that has sometimes been exhibited by black elected leaders toward the black poor sector has been replicated in the Latino elite's attitude toward new immigrants, who are often poor and uneducated. Further complicating the means of bridging these two communities is the sharp and sometimes fierce divisions within the Latino community where national identities are often more important than a sense of a Latino background. The various nations from which U.S. Latinos come constitute a wide breadth of ideological, political, cultural, and historical circumstances; it is difficult, at times, to actually speak of one Latino community. This means that black leaders must not only understand the general issues of language and immigration that impact all Hispanics, but must also struggle to grasp the individual national politics that emerge within the Latino community as it seeks allies and unity with non-Latinos.

These differences have played and continue to play an important role in Washington, D.C., due to the presence of so many national Latino groupings in the city. From the usually conservative Cuban community to the mostly undocumented but growing Salvadoran community, national and political differences have conditioned the African American response, ability, and desire for unity. However, if the proper lessons and insights are drawn from the political events of recent years, then the possibility, and recognition of the necessity, for finding what Jesse Jackson calls "common ground" can emerge.

NOTES

1. "Indices: A Statistical Index to District of Columbia 1992" (Washington, D.C.: District of Columbia Government), p. 81.

2. Ibid.

3. For a fuller analysis of the role of the United States in El Salvador, see Warner Poelchu, ed., *White Paper Whitewash: Interviews with Philip Agree on the CIA and El Salvador* (New York: Deep Cover Books, 1981).

4. "Indices," op. cit., p. 81.

5. Ibid.

6. Ibid.

7. Mike Davis, "Who Killed LA?: The War Against the Cities," *Crossroads* (June 1993), p. 7.

8. Ibid.

9. Ibid.

10. Eunice S. Grier, "The Changing Population of the District of Columbia" (Washington, D.C.: Greater Washington Research Center, 1990), pp. 29–30.

11. *Racial and Ethnic Tensions in American Communities: Poverty, Inequality, and Discrimination, Vol. I: The Mount Pleasant Report* (Washington, D.C.: U.S. Commission on Civil Rights, January 1993), p. 9. (Hereafter cited as Commission Report.)

12. Ibid., pp. 46, 76.

13. At many of the more affluent establishments it is possible for a waiter to earn as much as $40,000 per year. While this challenges conventional wisdom that all service jobs are low paying, it should be noted here that this constitutes only a limited number of jobs, and most of these jobs are held by whites.

14. Andrew Hacker, *Two Nations: Black and White, Separate, Hostile, Unequal* (New York: Charles Scribner's Sons, 1992), p. 114.

15. Commission Report, p. 82.

16. Clarence Lusane, "Police Bullet Explodes Community's Frustration," *Guardian* (May 22, 1991), p. 3.

17. Ola Alston and Mike Zielinski, "U.S. War on Salvador Comes to D.C. Streets," *Guardian* (May 21, 1991), p. 4.

18. Commission Report, p. iii.

19. Elsa Walsh, "Shaffer-Corona Is Indicted on Theft Charge," *Washington Post* (February 11, 1987).

20. Nell Henderson, "Power at the Ballot Box Eludes D.C. Hispanics; Task Force Attempts to Bridge the Gap," *Washington Post* (May 5, 1992), p. A1.

21. Arthur A. Fletcher, Letter of Transmittal, January 1993, cited in Commission Report.

22. Commission Report, p. 149.

23. Ibid., pp. 141–142.

24. Ibid., p. 143.

25. Ibid., p. 10.

26. Interview with the Coalition for African American and Latino Unity leader Kemba Maish, July 22, 1993, and CAALU brochure.

27. Arturo Griffiths and Benito Bolden, Citywide Multicultural Leadership Summit Final Report (December 1992), p. 1.

28. Ibid., p. 37.

29. Interview with Arturo Griffiths, July 23, 1993.

6

Generating Racial and Ethnic Conflict in Miami: Impact of American Foreign Policy and Domestic Racism

Daryl Harris

Except for Native Americans, every identifiable ethnic and racial group in the United States has origins outside of the United States. While immigration per se is certainly not new, what is discernible about the newer (post-1960) immigrants is their place of origin. Increasingly, many immigrants trace their origins to places other than Europe, with considerable numbers of people coming from countries south of the U.S./Mexican border.[1]

The reception that immigrants receive upon entry or attempted entry into the United States depends largely upon how they are classified by immigration policy. Since "All societies are simultaneously political and economic,"[2] this distinction is ambiguous, thus rendering the official classification scheme arbitrary. A "political immigrant" classification versus an "economic immigrant" classification can and generally does generate divergent treatment from the receiving government. At best, having the former classification—as is the case with many of the Cuban immigrants in Miami—can entitle group members to substantial assistance packages from the host government. By contrast, having the latter classification—as is the case currently with many Haitians attempting to migrate to the United States—can result in group members being turned away on the high seas.

With regard to Cuban immigrants, the political classification status they acquired enabled them to enter the United States with considerable and favorable alternatives and options, so that over the long term they were able to establish viable institutions and support networks for group members. This was made possible partly because the start of their rapid influx into the United States came at the height of cold war politics between the Soviet-led East and U.S.-led West. With the Castro-inspired Cuban socialist revolution intensifying the East/West ideological contest for global preeminence, the Cuban émigrés evolved a symbolic political status beneficial to both the American government and Soviet-supported Cuban government. Together the two governments formulated and implemented special accords allowing for the Cuban exodus to the United States, thus ensuring that beneficial outcomes would be bestowed upon each side.[3]

Addressing the political and functional purposes of the Cuban migration to the United States, political scientist Silvia Pedraza-Bailey maintains that,

In America, all the political migrations that took place during the peak years of the Cold War—the Hungarians, Berliners, and Cubans—served an important symbolic function. In this historical period of the Cold War, West and East contested the superiority of their political and economic systems. Political immigrants who succeeded in the flight to freedom became touching symbols around which to weave the legitimacy needed for foreign policy.[4]

With foreign policy objectives attended to, the American government embarked on a massive program aimed at easing the Cuban immigrants' transition into the country and advancing their political-economic and social interests. Thus the cumulative successes of white Cubans in the Miami community are linked directly to a wide range of public assistance programs, programs that are now regularly and vigorously challenged when blacks are the proposed beneficiaries. Ironically, many of the white Cubans who benefited immensely from U.S. governmental assistance programs in the 1960s are today's most ardent opponents of liberalized governmental programs required to significantly improve the condition of blacks in urban America.

To facilitate the Cubans' structural assimilation into the United States the Cuban Refugee Emergency Center was created in 1960 by President Dwight D. Eisenhower. Its initial function was to handle the resettlement of new immigrants in Miami. Shortly thereafter, President John F. Kennedy directed the Cuban Refugee Program (CRP) to proceed with the resettlement process, thereby enabling many to obtain food, clothing, housing services, health care services, jobs, transportation and adjustment support, educational opportunities, and other services. From 1961 through 1973, approximately $957.1 million was expended on the program, reaching an estimated 80 percent of Cuban immigrants. Moreover, the U.S. government instituted bilingual educational programs and provided retraining services for former doctors, lawyers, social workers, and other professionals. Through 1972, the federal government spent in excess of $130 million on various special programs designed to expedite the transition process.[5]

Prior to Fidel Castro's rise to power, the Cuban immigrant population in the United States was negligible. Pre-1959 figures indicate that an estimated 30,000 Cubans resided in the United States. Between 1959 and 1980, however, over 800,000 Cubans departed their homeland in search of freedoms they felt were being curtailed by the Castro regime.[6]

Despite efforts by the federal government to relocate the Cuban émigrés throughout the United States the vast amount eventually resettled in the Miami community. Given that the federal government vigorously formulated a broad range of assistance programs for the hundreds of thousands of new Cuban residents, is it not reasonable to expect that this would create an immense feeling of disillusionment among Miami's "indigenous" residents—black *and* white? Moreover, given that this immigration explosion commenced at a time when Miami's black population stood at the threshold of qualitative political-economic gains resulting from the civil rights movement, is it not also reasonable to expect Miami's blacks to feel particularly aggrieved? In the face of unremitting subordination at the hands of white policymakers, blacks were accorded the unenviable position of watching newcomers being granted precisely what they had been attempting to secure for themselves: the uninterrupted opportunity to develop viable, life-sustaining institutions.

In areas ranging from employment opportunities to housing availability, the relocation of the hundreds of thousands of immigrants from points south of Florida served only to deepen the historic interracial problems in Miami. Perhaps the area most heavily affected by the new residents was employment; as expected, its implications for black employment prospects were catastrophic. Because of the service-oriented economy of Miami, area businesses participated in the practice of using low-skilled immigrant labor, at lower wages of course, to obstruct the demands of indigenous labor.

According to a 1963 commentary the estimated 100,000 Cubans who descended on the Miami community in the first few years of that decade magnified tensions among the community's racial and ethnic groups, and in some ways spawned a number of new social and economic problems; this process resulted in the development of a contentious and potentially explosive alignment of "native" Americans against "them."[7] The report concluded that in all areas of the city's life the new immigrants caused considerable discord. The area's black leadership establishment, including James Whitehead, leader of the city's Urban League, lamented over the realization that the Cuban immigrants were accorded the same privileges as whites at a time when blacks were still being denied such liberties simply because of skin color.

Examples of this disparate treatment were evidenced in the policies of county schools, for instance, where special classes were developed to accommodate the language difficulties of Cuban children, while at the same time black children were prohibited from attending integrated schools. Given this, one could arguably reason that blacks would feel an acute sense of disaffection and resentment over their being denied fundamental liberties that were granted to people fresh off the high seas.

In the area of employment blacks and whites were displaced by Cuban immigrants who are willing to work at much lower wages. In 1963 it was estimated that over 90 percent of the area's garment industry workers were Cubans, an astonishingly high percentage for a relatively recent immigrant group.[8] This would remain almost unchanged well into the 1970s, at which time an estimated 85 percent of the clothing industry's factory workers were Cuban.[9] Remarks and analyses from notable leaders in the Miami community confirm some of the implications related to the immigration process in 1963. Robert Gladnick, a union business manager, was quoted as saying:

The entire garment industry of Miami employs 6,300. The non-union shops are staffed 98 percent by Cubans. Since the industry expanded, between 1,000 and 1,500 new jobs were created and they all went to Cubans. The arrival of the Cubans definitely stopped the progress of the Negro in the industry. The Negroes were about to make a breakthrough as stewards when the Cubans came in. We feel the problem of the Cuban refugees with great compassion, but the employer is the real chiseler. The employer wants cheap labor. The Cubans will work for less than the Negroes will. The Negro therefore becomes the victim.[10]

Gladnick's reference that employers in the Miami community are largely responsible for creating the area's seething ethnic and racial atmosphere is only partially correct. A more complete accounting would implicate the local business community along with the host of governmental and civic entities. All contributed to the elevation of the immigrant Cuban community; all conformed to the practice of disregard, neglect, and subordination of the area's black population.

To charge only the immigrant Cuban group for the tense ethnic/racial problems in Miami blurs one's understanding of the historical patterns of race relations. Though many in Miami's white Cuban population might now conform to some American myths and concepts—racial, economic, political, or otherwise—they were not the original architects of Miami's racial disparities and injustices. This point was noted by C. Gaylord Rolle, a prominent local leader and newspaper publisher, who in 1963 said:

The coming of the Cubans has accentuated the crisis of Miami's Negro population and definitely intensified unemployment. But social injustice existed before they got here. Over 12,000 Negroes in the county have lost jobs since the Cuban migration began.[11]

Miami's changing population profile provides a clue as to why tensions developed over competition for residential space, jobs, economic development, and political influence and viability. In 1950, the share of the total population of Miami that was born in one of the Latin American countries was 1 percent; the black share was 13 percent. By 1960 when the population changes began to become noticeable as a result of the Castro revolution, the Latin

American–born population living in Miami rose to an estimated 7 percent; the black share increased modestly to 15 percent. By 1970, however, Hispanics comprised 21 percent of Miami's population, whereas the black share remained at its 1960 level of 15 percent.[12] The two decades preceding the 1980 black rebellion saw approximately 70 percent of the population growth in the Miami community attributed to Latinos.[13] In just twenty years, the demographic landscape of Miami had become increasingly Hispanic, with white Cubans constituting the bulk of that group's population. According to Raymond Mohl, "by the early 1970s, Miami had become the world's second largest Cuban city, smaller only than Havana."[14]

In a total population of 1,625,781 in the Miami Standard Metropolitan Statistical Area (SMSA) in 1980, 580,025 or 35 percent were of Hispanic origin, and 405,810 or 70 percent of those were classified as Cuban. These data do not include the estimated 125,000 Cubans who migrated directly to Miami during the famous 1980 Mariel boatlift. By 1990 Hispanics constituted 49 percent of the population in the Miami SMSA, increasing to 953,407 out of a total of 1,937,094. The 1990 Cuban share of the Hispanic portion stood at 563,979 or 59 percent. Because the black share of the Hispanic origin population is small—only 10,167 in 1980 and 28,372 in 1990—it is apparent that the racial character of Miami's Cuban population is predominantly white. In 1990 the non-Hispanic black population was 397,993 or 20 percent of the total. In 1980 the white Cuban population outnumbered the black population by almost a two-to-one margin, although by 1990 the numerical difference was not as great.[15] However, when other Hispanics in the Miami community—such as Mexicans, Venezuelans, Colombians, and Nicaraguans—are taken into consideration, the racial-demographic divide becomes even more striking.

Still, it was primarily white Cubans who migrated to Miami during the early 1960s and established this city as a place where persons of Hispanic descent could find refuge. It was the early Cuban immigrants, many of whom were highly skilled and accomplished professionals before they arrived in Miami, who, aided to some degree by governmental assistance packages, were instrumental in transforming Miami into a flourishing tourist, trade, and banking center. The early white Cuban migrants, who currently form the upper economic and political echelon of Miami's Hispanic community, are the ones who determine the essence of Hispanic politics in Miami.[16]

Various indicators of business activity show the Hispanic community surpassing the black community by considerable margins. Whereas Hispanics owned and operated approximately 30 banks and nearly 16,000 area businesses by 1986, in the early 1980s black-owned businesses comprised only 1 percent of Miami's businesses, and 88 percent of those were owner-operated with no employees. It does appear that much of the entrepreneurial success of Cuban businesspersons came at the expense of black-owned firms. For instance, in 1960 blacks owned 25 percent of Dade County gas stations, but by 1979 the black total had plummeted to 9 percent, whereas Hispanic ownership reached 48 percent of the total.[17]

Part of this dissimilar pattern of business growth can be explained by a cursory view of lending practices by the Small Business Administration. Of the nearly $100 million it distributed to area businesses between 1968 and 1979, blacks received a paltry 6.4 percent of the total, Hispanics received 47 percent, and non-Hispanic whites got 46.5 percent.[18] Considered in its totality black economic development fared measurably worse than that of other groups in the Miami community because of a combination of institutional and systemic—political, societal, and structural—forces (historical and contemporary), which, when viewed forthrightly, demonstrate a pattern ranging from invidious racial subjugation to the more clandestine, but no less effective, policy choice of abdicating responsibility for the black predicament.

Compounding the adverse perceptions and socioeconomic ramifications that the immigration of white Cubans had on the black community was another dimension of the immigration issue that served to sharpen blacks' sense of injustice and disaffection: the apparent contradictory immigration policy of denying *black* Haitians asylum while simultaneously granting it to Cubans. This inconsistency became disturbingly vivid to black Miamians when, during the Cuban Mariel boatlift, tens of thousands of Haitians also arrived in the Miami area. In spite of detailed accounts of atrocities from individuals who had been persecuted, imprisoned, and/or tortured by Haitian authorities under the U.S.-sanctioned Duvalier regime, the U.S. Immigration Department refused to grant fleeing Haitians refuge on the grounds that they were fleeing Haiti for economic reasons, rather than political reasons, which are supposedly the basis for gaining asylum status.

A major consequence of this dual, contradictory policy was that it fostered a heightened sense among black Miamians that justice and fairness in the American social system are elusive propositions, not only for their "indigenous" members but also for all persons of African descent. Whereas in some major urban centers throughout the United States disfranchised and disaffected blacks and Hispanics might together form a basis for a compelling political coalition to reckon with, no such development has ever existed in Miami.[19] Instead of being viewed as a potential ally in the cause of minority rights, empowerment, and justice, Miami's Hispanics, mainly because of the strength of the white Cuban middle and upper classes in conjunction with their sheer numbers in the Miami community, are viewed by many blacks with suspicion and as disrupters of black economic and political progress.

Yet while the influx of the nearly one million Cuban and Hispanic immigrants may have served to intensify black discontent in Miami, another underlying source of black disaffection is to be found in the relationship that blacks have with whites and the white-controlled governmental institutions. Black attempts to acquire the type of power that may be beneficial to improving the life conditions of the area's black population are frustrated by the local governmental structure and election systems. Perhaps the most conspicuous characteristic of Dade County's governmental structure is in its makeup of municipalities. Although metropolitan Dade County has twenty-seven cities, the predominantly Hispanic cities of Miami and Hialeah being the first and second largest, respectively, there exists within the county large concentrations of black people (60 percent) who are surprisingly, yet systematically excluded from any of the county's twenty-seven municipalities.[20] The most obvious political implication of this conscious political subterfuge is that it eliminates from electoral competition substantial blocs of black voters who could determine the outcomes of important contests. Reduced to an ineffectual political status, blacks living in unincorporated areas repeatedly observe that their concerns get moved to the back burner of the institutional agenda. It is likely that this government-created predicament either engenders or heightens the feeling of disaffection and discontent among Miami's black population.

The area comprising Liberty City and surrounding neighborhoods, the site of much of the violence during 1980, provides a fitting example of how the state uses disfranchisement procedures to deprive black people of self-determination and potential electoral leverage in the formal political system.[21] In the early 1980s, this forsaken 15.3 square mile unincorporated area had a population of approximately 103,500 people, some 70 percent of which were black, 14 percent Hispanic, and 18 percent other. All were subject to the jurisdiction of the county government. And because county public policymakers were generally perceived as neglecting this area, community activists devised and promulgated a plan to turn this largely economically depressed area into an independent city, with all of the functions and privileges accorded to any city.[22] The proposed "New City" would have been the third largest city in the county, but was rejected by the county commission.

In his promotion of the "New City" concept, C. Gaylord Rolle, publisher of *Liberty News* and architect of the idea in the 1960s, declared, "We want a divorce from Metro." "The Grounds?" he mused: "Cruel and inhumane treatment. Incompatibility. They don't love our children."[23] Although the proposition eventually fizzled, the sustained promotion of it for nearly two decades by many of the county's most prominent black leaders illustrated much of what was, and still is, wrong with the county's governmental structure: it has an obstructionist effect on the ability of unincorporated black county's residents to determine policy affecting their lives. In effect, under this structure, the very foundation of government is directly responsible for severing the voices of 60 percent or approximately 163,000 black Dade County residents, nearly one-half or 70,000 of them living in the proposed "New City" area alone.

Compounding this conscious disfranchisement policy has been the continued use of electoral systems, most notably the at-large and second primary systems, which have the effect of diluting black voter strength and thereby suppressing black electoral leverage in the political system. Numerous studies have shown that the at-large electoral system in particular is an effective impediment to black political (numerically speaking) empowerment.[24] At-large electoral systems act as a means of diluting the votes of groups—racial or political—and subsequently severely restricting the ability of the group under observation to elect members of its choice to highly valued elected positions. The runoff electoral arrangement has similar consequences. Under this system, instead of needing a mere plurality, candidates are required to receive an absolute majority of votes (50 percent plus one) in the primary in order to win. Failure to get the absolute majority forces the two top vote-getters into a second primary. Thus under this electoral arrangement, jurisdictions with significant, but less than majority, black populations subject strong first-round black candidates to the tangles of racial bloc-voting politics.[25] This electoral arrangement is featured only in the South.

As with various dilutionary systems currently in operation, there is nothing in the wording of at-large and second primary systems to suggest that they are discriminatory. However, the essence of vote dilution is that it is a group phenomenon and "occurs because the propensity of an identifiable" racial or political "group to vote as a bloc waters down the voting strength of another identifiable" racial or political group, within certain contexts. Moreover, "vote dilution often operates to diminish a group's potential voting strength that derives from the group's" numerical strength and geographic concentration.[26]

The diminished political power resulting from vote dilution is not the result of the behavior of the group whose votes are diluted. In other words, it is not that black people are apolitical or politically inept; rather, it is the political procedures and practices designed by the majority group, combined with the bloc voting of the majority group(s), that operate in a dilute and discriminatory fashion on the numerically smaller black group. Ultimately this translates into limited or marginal political power for blacks in the Miami area. "To say that a group's votes are diluted implies that the ineffectiveness of its ballots is beyond its control" and that the causes are systemic.[27]

The existence of the at-large and second primary electoral system in Dade County and Miami invariably has meant that black concerns have been subject to the sanction of elements outside the black community, most notably the prominent Anglo and Hispanic political and business leadership. The net result of this external stranglehold on the black community has meant that the most progressive voices within the black community have had greater difficulties winning citywide and countywide offices. By contrast, the more moderate elements in the black community are often projected as "leaders," and on occasion are provided with a platform—elected or appointed—to articulate their accommodationist agendas. Under this arrangement, black elected leadership becomes more symbol than substance for urban blacks, especially for those who live in Dade County's underdeveloped and systematically disfranchised, unincorporated areas.

Until recently, the at-large electoral system held sway for Dade County Commission races. However, as a result of recent litigation—*Meek et al. v. Metropolitan Dade County, Florida, et al.* (1993)—filed by black and Hispanic leaders against the county, the at-large electoral procedure has been prohibited as a means of electing county commissioners. Replacing the nine-member County Commission, where commissioners were elected at-large, is a thirteen-member district system, where commissioners are elected from individual districts. Special elections were held in March and April 1993 to choose the new county commission. Filling the thirteen seats are six Hispanics, four blacks, and three Anglos.[28] This change is significant insofar as it ensures that both blacks and Hispanics will be elected to the Dade County Commission, whereas prior to the system change, electoral efforts on the part of both groups were continually frustrated. The system change, however, applies only to the County Commission. Municipalities in Dade County, such as Miami, and other county elective offices are not required to comply.

BLACK URBAN COLLECTIVE VIOLENCE IN MIAMI

In all likelihood the actualization of black urban collective violence in Miami that began in 1980 probably would not have occurred had it not been for the long train of abuses meted out to blacks by authorities representing the political-legal system.

These include not only police killings of black men and other police transgressions against members of the black community, but also the repeated failures of the political-legal system to dispense justice when black people were the complainants. The continued failures of the democratic process to exact justice, especially in the highly charged and visible cases that had definite racial overtones, may have provided some blacks with the psychological basis to finally sever what remaining faith they may have had in the area's political-economic and judicial systems to execute policies and laws justly, impartially, and equitably. Though intergroup relations in Miami have generally been sour, with blacks bearing the brunt of institutional abuses, it was the cumulative impact of political-legal improprieties and insensitivities that represented the "last straw" that broke the area's tenuous hold on intergroup tranquility.

Leading up the 1980 racial conflagration, Miami's blacks had been treated to a series of highly visible and disparaging incidents that infuriated members of the black community, causing practically the entire community to question the legitimacy of the political system and to doubt the veracity of white political and public leadership. These incidents simply reinforced an already widely held perception among blacks that the political-legal system is flawed and treats them unfairly, especially in comparison with Latinos.

The case that blew the lid off of the tense racial-ethnic pressure cooker was the police killing of Arthur McDuffie and the complete exoneration of the four white officers so charged.[29] On December 16, 1979, after apparently violating a traffic law while riding his motorcycle, McDuffie was—in the course of events that followed—pursued by at least a dozen police cars. When the pursuit ended, McDuffie was violently set upon by as many as twelve officers, some striking him over his head with their Kelites (heavy eighteen-inch flashlights). When the free-for-all ended, McDuffie lay unconscious, and died soon thereafter.

For many blacks in Miami, the trial, which was moved to Tampa and heard by an all-white jury, sharply defined and reaffirmed their subordinate racial status in relation to institutions of authority, power, and other non-European groups. And when the "not guilty" verdicts were read, after only two hours and forty-five minutes of deliberation, that perception of subordination because of injustice was promptly confirmed. After waiting for the wheels of jurisprudence to execute justice, only to see that the process was unresponsive to even their most obvious of claims, some blacks resorted to what would become known as the most serious instance of black urban violence since the mid- to late 1960s. In each succeeding instance of black urban violence in Miami during the 1980s, the immediate precipitant was some form of police violence against members of the black community.

CONCLUSION

Although not an exhaustive presentation of every conceivable causal influence, this chapter has surveyed a number of developments and determinants that played an important role in shaping the content of intergroup relations in Miami. It was suggested that both foreign policy and local government activities contributed to the volatility of racial and ethnic tensions in Miami and played a role in the actualization of black urban violence.

The immigration process is an important factor to consider for at least two reasons. First, it drastically transformed the particulars, if not the substance, of intergroup relations in Miami. Because the migration of Hispanics, particularly white Cubans, commenced and accelerated at a time when blacks stood at the threshold of qualitative political and economic gains attributable to the 1960s civil rights and black freedom movements, blacks were adversely affected in numerous areas of living, including employment and housing. Moreover, the host of governmental and civic organizations that made it possible for white Cubans to establish viable, life-sustaining institutions and communities remained relatively irresolute in providing community assistance packages to the city's indigenous black population.

At the core of urban black Miami's discontent and disaffection is its continued material subordination. In surveys of socioeconomic status indicators, not only is the black community ranked behind other groups in the Miami community, but in some areas such as poor housing and high unemployment, exceptionally high percentages of blacks suffer disproportionately in terms of the total populations.

Compounding the high levels of blacks' material subordination is their relative political powerlessness. Sources identified in this chapter that contribute to this predicament are Miami's governmental structure, which systematically excludes 60 percent of Miami's black population from incorporated jurisdictions, and that structure's use of electoral systems—at-large and second primary—that dilute black votes and therefore suppress black electoral influence. Although Dade County Commission elections were recently changed from an at-large system to a district system, taken together, these mechanisms effectively eliminated most of Miami's black population from meaningful electoral competition and participation up until the spring of 1993.

Lastly, the cumulative impact of political-legal transgressions against members of the black community and the subsequent failure of the judicial system to exact results acceptable to many blacks together represent the decisive elements that triggered the violent insurgency movements in the 1980s. Due to many transgressions, including the McDuffie episode, blacks increasingly questioned the ability of the "system" to legitimately apply its laws fairly. Blacks also perceived Latinos as benefiting, politically and economically, from this system's relationship to and oppression of blacks.

NOTES

1. Alejandro Portes and Robert L. Bach, *Latin Journey: Cuban and Mexican Immigrants in the United States* (Berkeley: University of California Press, 1985), p. 71.

2. Silvia Pedraza-Bailey, *Political and Economic Migrants in America: Cubans and Mexicans* (Austin: University of Texas Press, 1985), p. 11.

3. Ibid., p. 17.

4. Ibid., pp. 17–18.

5. Ibid., pp. 40–45.

6. Portes and Bach, op. cit., pp. 84–85.

7. Allan Morrison, "Miami's Cuban Refugee Crisis," *Ebony* 18 (June 1963), p. 97.

8. Ibid., pp. 97–98.

9. David B. Longbrake and Woodrow W. Nichols, Jr., *Sunshine and Shadows in Metropolitan Miami* (Cambridge, Mass.: Ballinger Publishing, 1976), p. 50.

10. Morrison, op. cit., p. 98.

11. Ibid., p. 100.

12. Morton D. Winsberg, "Ethnic Competition for Residential Space in Miami, Florida, 1970–80," *American Journal of Economics and Sociology* 42 (July 1983), pp. 306–307.

13. United States Commission on Civil Rights, *Confronting Racial Isolation in Miami* (Washington, D.C.: Government Printing Office, 1982), p. 3.

14. Raymond A. Mohl, "Miami: The Ethnic Cauldron," in Richard M. Bernard and Bradley R. Rice, eds., *Sunbelt Cities: Politics and Growth Since World War II* (Austin: University of Texas Press, 1983), p. 70.

15. U.S. Bureau of the Census, *Florida Census of Population* (Washington, D.C., 1980), pp. 11, 49; U.S. Bureau of the Census, *1990 Census of Population, General Population Characteristics, Florida* (Washington, D.C., June 1992), Sec. 1 of 2, p. 24.

16. Pedraza-Bailey, op. cit., p. 11; U.S. Commission on Civil Rights, *Confronting Racial Isolation*, pp. 10–18; Christopher L. Warren, John F. Stack, Jr., and John G. Corbett, "Minority Mobilization in an International City: Rivalry and Conflict in Miami," *PS* 19 (Summer 1986), p. 628.

17. Raymond Mohl, "On the Edge: Blacks and Hispanics in Metropolitan Miami Since 1959," *Florida Historical Quarterly* 59 (July 1990), pp. 45–46.

18. Ibid., pp. 45–46; Warren et al., op. cit., p. 629.

19. For a discussion on the possibilities of blacks and Hispanics forming political coalitions, see Ira Katznelson, *City Trenches: Urban Politics and the Patterning of Class in the United States* (New York: Pantheon, 1981).

20. Warren et al., op. cit., p. 629.

21. Deil S. Wright, *Understanding Intergovernmental Relations*, 3d ed. (Pacific Grove, CA: Brooks/Cole Publishing, 1988). On p. 40, Wright discusses "Dillon's Rule," named for an Iowa judge who in the 1860s provided the parameters around which state and local governments interact. The essence of their relationship is that localities are subject to the will of state legislatures (barring constitutional limitations), and there is no common-law right of local self-government.

22. The New City Political Action Committee, "Tentative Budget of the Proposed New City—FY 1982–83," reported submitted to Dade County Commission, September 1981.

23. *The Miami Herald*, April 14, 1981, p. 3B.

24. Numerous chapters analyzing the negative effect that the at-large election system has on the black electoral prospect appear in Chandler Davidson, ed., *Minority Vote Dilution* (Washington, D.C.: Howard University Press, 1984); see also Clinton Jones, "The Impact of Local Election Systems on Black Political Representation," *Urban Affairs Quarterly*, vol. 11, no. 3 (March 1976): 345–356.

25. "Special Report on Second Primaries," *Focus* (Joint Center for Political Studies), vol. 12, no. 6 (June 1984): 5.

26. Chandler Davidson, "Minority Vote Dilution: An Overview," in Davidson, op. cit., p. 4.

27. Ibid., pp. 4–5.

28. *Meek et al. v. Metropolitan Dade County, Fla. et al.*, 985 F.2d 1471(11th Cir. 1993); *County News*, vol. 25, no. 10, May 24, 1993, p. 15.

29. See "T ime For Stronger Charges in McDuffie Case," *Miami Times*, January 31, 1980, p. 4; "Dead: One Black Man's Disease: Rampant Racism," *Miami Times*, January 3, 1980, p. 5; "Manslaughter Charge Just Don't Get It," *Miami Times*, January 3, 1980, p. 4; also see Bruce Porter and Marvin Dunn, *The Miami Riots of 1980: Crossing the Bounds* (Lexington, Mass.: D. C. Heath, 1984), pp. 33–43.

7

Blacks and Koreans in Los Angeles: The Case of LaTasha Harlins and Soon Ja Du

Karen Umemoto

The emergence of global cities such as Los Angeles has added new complexities to the topic of interethnic relations. The international migration of labor, migratory family reunification, and forced displacement by war or poverty have created cities with multiple levels of socioeconomic stratification and multiple arenas of racial, ethnic, and class conflict. The conflict between Korean Americans and African Americans, neither of whom enjoy economic, political, social, or cultural parity with whites in the United States, is indicative of the increase in conflict between two subordinate but unequal groups.

On March 16, 1991, LaTasha Harlins, a 15-year-old African American girl, was shot and killed by Soon Ja Du, a Korean merchant in South Los Angeles. There are conflicting interpretations of what transpired in their confrontation. There is, however, videotaped evidence of a scuffle between the two followed by a gunshot fired to the back of LaTasha Harlins's head as she was walking away from Soon Ja Du. The decision of the presiding judge not to impose prison time raised anger within the African American community and fear of backlash in the Korean American community. This tragic incident and the judicial process that followed escalated the ongoing tensions between Koreans and African Americans and was seen as a setback to reconciliation efforts among organizational leaders within the two ethnic communities.

The incident and the judicial process were perceived differently in each community. Why, and how? A comparison of the two ethnic newspapers reveals a difference in the way in which two events, the killing of LaTasha Harlins and the trial of Soon Ja Du, can be perceived and interpreted. This difference has implications for current methods and approaches to conflict resolution between communities of color. The framing of the events also reveals a connection with the controversial Los Angeles police beating of Rodney King, especially as seen through the African American community-based newspaper, the *Los Angeles Sentinel*, and may help to explain the interconnectedness between the two cases. The thematic shift of the *Los Angeles Sentinel* coverage of the LaTasha Harlins case from an issue of "disrespect" by Koreans toward African Americans to an issue of "injustice" at the sentencing of Soon Ja Du without imprisonment marked an escalation of tensions and a closer association with the Rodney King case. The emergence of the theme of scapegoating in the *Korea Times* presents a contrasting interpretive framing of the case.

DEMOGRAPHIC BACKDROP

There has been an extremely rapid rate of demographic change in the racial composition of Los Angeles due to the increase in Latino and Asian populations and the simultaneous decrease in the white and African American populations. The proportion of African Americans in Los Angeles County declined from 12.4 percent to 11.2 percent between 1980 and 1990. The Asian American population, meanwhile, increased from 5.9 percent of Los Angeles County in 1980 to 10.7 percent in 1990. Latinos, who comprise 40 percent of Los Angeles, also increased in large numbers with a 71 percent increase between 1980 and 1990.[1]

The growth of the Asian and Latino populations is greatly due to the entrance of immigrants to Los Angeles. African American migration from the South took place mainly during World War II, though African Americans have been present in Los Angeles since its founding. The Korean American community in Los Angeles was initially established in the early 1900s, but greatly expanded after the Immigration Act of 1965. The number of Koreans increased 140 percent between 1980 and 1990 alone, from 60,618 to 145,431 persons. Los Angeles' Koreatown is presently home to the largest concentration of Koreans in the United States. Mexicans preceded all groups in the settlement of Los Angeles, as Los Angeles was built on what was part of Mexico before the annexation of the Southwest following the Mexican American War of 1848. The recent increase in Latinos includes primarily Mexican immigrants, but also others from Central and South America. The rapid rate of population increase among Asians and Latinos, and especially among immigrants, has drastically changed the character of many neighborhoods, including many historically African American communities. This has contributed to tension as individuals and ethnically based institutions have come to compete in the labor market, in political elections, and in other arenas.

The current economic status of Asian American and African American groups differ significantly. The economic status of Asian Americans is higher than African Americans in Los Angeles, but lower than whites in Los Angeles County. The 1990 median per capita income, for example, of an African American was $12,018, well below the $16,149 per capita income averaged across the county. County poverty rates also differ between African Americans, Asian Americans, and whites, with rates of 24 percent, 14 percent, and 12.5 percent respectively.[2]

The economic problems faced by African Americans in inner-city areas are even more severe with an estimated 25 percent of African American adults and 50 percent of African American youth in Los Angeles city detached from the labor force. Paul Ong and others describe a process of cumulative causality in the economic decline in ghetto neighborhoods. Many African Americans have remained trapped in low-wage jobs due to discrimination and the decline in higher paid industrial jobs. Some have, over generations, opted to drop out of the labor force or enter the informal or underground economies.[3] Nationally, elimination of affirmative action quotas in employment, reduction of public-sector jobs, change in skill demands in the central cities, and residential segregation have been cited for the serious economic decline of African Americans in the inner cities.[4] Though Koreans and other Asian Americans earn more, on average, than African Americans, Asians in the inner city also face harsh economic conditions. For instance, about half of all Koreans who live in inner-city areas of Los Angeles earn less than $15,000 annually.[5]

The social history that accompanies the economic trend is also different for each ethnic community. The long struggle for civil rights and "black power" did not translate into the dreams that leaders such as Martin Luther King, Jr., or Malcolm X spoke of. The persistent poverty and inner-city decline since that period has led to a greater frustration with the political system that was expected by some to mediate change. Many African American youth have expressed disillusionment with the economy, polity, and educational system through rap and other cultural expression. The belief that immigrants take housing and jobs away from native workers, as well as the "model minority" stereotypes of Asian Americans, has created social distance among some African Americans and others toward Asian Americans.[6]

An idyllic image of America has been promoted in Korea since the United States' involvement in the Korean War and only now is beginning to fade as return migrants are bringing back more sober images of their experiences in America. Most Korean immigrant entrepreneurs are college educated and have felt frustration with their inability to transfer their skills to the United States labor market due to language, licensing, and other barriers. They have seen few options and have opened family-run businesses with capital brought from Korea or pooled capital from formal and informal institutions. Carrying stereotypes that originated from Western media images in Korea and lacking a fuller understanding of American history, some Koreans have blamed African Americans for not being able to "pull themselves up by the bootstraps" as they themselves may feel they have done.[7]

Like Jewish merchants before them, Korean merchants in south-central Los Angeles have been criticized by some African Americans for the lack of capital and social investment by Koreans in the African American community beyond that invested directly in their business enterprises. Even though there are numerically more African American-owned businesses in the Los Angeles metropolitan area than Korean-owned businesses (23,932 as compared to 17,165 businesses respectively in 1987), proportionately, the rate of entrepreneurship is higher among Koreans.[8] Additionally, Korean merchants are visibly present, as few live in south or south-central Los Angeles and many other business owners have left the area. The NAACP estimates that Koreans own about one-third of the area's small markets and liquor stores.[9]

Korean business in these areas of the city, however, tend to be undercapitalized and characterized by low profit rates, especially compared to those businesses located in more affluent areas. There tends to be a higher turnover in ownership in south-central Los Angeles since many small business enterprises leave when they have enough capital to relocate to more lucrative areas with lower crime rates. The transience of businesses has hindered the nurturing of more numerous long-term reciprocal relationships between Korean merchants and African American customers. The difficulties leading to the low rate of African American entrepreneurship—cultural and language differences, the use of unpaid Korean family labor over the hiring of local residents, and the high rate of crime—have fueled tensions between a number of local African American residents and Korean merchants.

The impact of demographic and economic changes on political contests are also affecting interethnic relations. African Americans have been deeply involved in electoral politics and have established relatively strong electoral bases. There are a significant number of locally elected African American officials in city, state, and federal offices. African American representation, however, has generally failed to translate into political or economic empowerment for African Americans despite—until 1993—the 20-year mayoral tenure of African American mayor Tom Bradley. Instead, there have been signs of increased disillusionment with the electoral system, especially among younger African Americans. In contrast, many Latinos and Asian Americans have increased their participation in the formal political system as demonstrated by the victories of Latino and Asian American candidates to the Los Angeles City Council and school board and the election of a Latina to the county board of supervisors during the late 1980s and early 1990s. Redistricting has allotted new seats to predominantly Latino districts, while decreasing the number of predominantly African American districts. The increasing visibility of Asian Americans and Latinos in the Republican party has also gained some attention among African Americans who are predominantly Democratic in their party affiliation.

These economic, political, and demographic changes are oc-
curring within the context of a changing global economy. Los
Angeles has become a global city—a meeting point between
transnational capital and labor on the rim of Pacific trade. These
profound changes have created new institutional and human
relationships. Theories of ethnic conflict have emphasized the
role of economic variables in the escalation of ethnic conflict.
Theories of domination, exploitation, competition, and hierarchy
have focused on the economic determinants of intergroup relations. While understanding the political economy of race and
ethnic relations is critical in understanding ethnic conflict, a
strictly materialist perspective leaves several unanswered questions. For example, there are many instances in which inequality
or exploitation may be evident along ethnic or racial boundaries,
but conflict is not visible. There are, in other words, instances of
cooperation as well as conflict between two subordinate groups.
The roles of perception, of ideology, and of identity as related to
economic or material conditions, but also as independent social
forces, are important to consider in order to understand the
variation of outcomes under similar economic conditions. The
following narrative media analysis of the news coverage of
events contained in the largest west coast African American and
English-language Korean American vernaculars provides a pre-
liminary look at the role of perception and interpretation in the
construction of ethnic and racial group identity, intergroup relations, and ethnic conflict.

SAME EVENT, DIFFERENT PERSPECTIVES

There is a striking contrast in the frames—the cumulative
explanatory pictures presented over time—of the *Sentinel* and the
Korea Times over the one-year coverage period studied between
March 1991 and March 1992. The *Los Angeles Sentinel* describes
the shooting of LaTasha Harlins as representative of the disrespect that Koreans allegedly have for African Americans. The
death of Harlins is placed in the context of complaints about
rudeness of merchants, their resistance to hiring African Americans, and high prices charged for merchandise in Korean-owned
stores. The theme of "disrespect" turns into "injustice" upon the

verdict and sentencing of Soon Ja Du, particularly upon the "no prison" sentence issued by Judge Joyce Karlin. The transition in the frame from the overriding theme of "disrespect" to one of "injustice" was accompanied by the construction of Soon Ja Du as an archetypal Korean merchant utilizing economic and political influence to collaborate with those in positions of power against the interests of African Americans, as represented by the plight of Harlins.

In contrast, the *Korea Times* presents the plight of Soon Ja Du as that of an archetypal Korean merchant who reportedly had been harassed for months by African American gang members and is pushed beyond her limits. She is reported to have accidentally fired a gun that she had never before used and allegedly never meant to use. She becomes symbolic of many Korean immigrants who work night and day in a new land in search of the American dream, only to find themselves victims of robberies in crime-ridden neighborhoods. Instead of a single archetype of African Americans, a distinction is made between African Americans who are actively fueling the scapegoating of Koreans and those who are willing to work together to avert it. As conflict intensifies between Korean merchants and individual African Americans, the focus shifts from the problem of "crime" to that of "anti-Korean hate crimes and scapegoating."

The change in frames from disrespect to injustice in the *Sentinel* and from crime to scapegoating in the *Korea Times* also represents a period of escalation of the conflict and coverage of the controversy. Overall, the media coverage of the shooting and the subsequent trial was much more focal to the *Korea Times* than the *Sentinel*. Many of the headlines in the *Sentinel* were dominated by the Rodney King beating, the trial of the LAPD officers accused of beating King, and related articles. Other reports—such as the legislative hearings on the appointment of Clarence Thomas to the Supreme Court, repeated cases of police brutality against African Americans, and the announcement by Magic Johnson of his contraction of the HIV virus—also contexualized the LaTasha Harlins case. The reporting of Soon Ja Du's shooting of LaTasha Harlins appeared in rhythmic beat with other tales of tragedy inflicted upon African Americans by circumstances beyond their control. A relationship with the Korean community was defined,

the relationship between African Americans and the
i more dominant institutions of society.

urrently, the reporting of the incident and subsequent
e. in the *Korea Times* was placed in the context of the quest to
attain the American dream. The centrality of the issue of Korean–
African American relations and the situation facing merchants was
even more pronounced in the *Korea Times*, given the size of the
newspaper in relation to the size of the *Sentinel*. The prominence of
the case may indicate the importance of Korean–African American
relations to the realization of their dreams.

LOS ANGELES SENTINEL: POLICE BRUTALITY, DISRESPECT, AND INJUSTICE AGAINST AFRICAN AMERICANS

The *Sentinel* coverage of the incident and subsequent trial was
positioned within a thematic context of injustice and was virtually situated alongside the issue of police brutality that dominated much of the headlines throughout the year, especially with
the beating of Rodney King taking place only several weeks
before the shooting of LaTasha Harlins. The initial report of the
incident was anchored by a photo of Shinese Harlins mourning
for her cousin LaTasha with an accompanying article, "Merchant
Charged: Teenager Shot, Killed in Dispute Over Orange Juice."[10]
The main headline above the photo and article called attention to
the pressure mounting for the resignation of LAPD Chief Daryl
Gates. Below the photograph were two other articles on the
Rodney King beating alongside another article about a "Man-
Beaten by Sheriffs Without 'Video Advantage.' " The contextualization of Harlins's death by the dominant issue of police brutality
gave the controversy between Koreans and African Americans
added resonance that became increasingly powerful as the trial
unfolded.

LaTasha Harlins's life became a personification of the African
American community's struggle against racism and "political
machinations going on behind closed doors," in reference to the
judicial case leading to the verdict.[11] In the pretrial period, the
main theme reported in the coverage of the LaTasha Harlins case
was that of "disrespect" toward African Americans on the part of
Korean businesspersons. In the first *Sentinel* article that described

the shooting, Soon Ja Du was portrayed as an unconscionable killer without guilt or remorse about what she had done.[12] In addition, two sets of articles appeared in the several months following the incident that, together, composed an archetype of the Korean merchant as unscrupulous and insensitive. Another article covered an incident where an African American man, Arthur Mitchell, was also shot and killed by another Korean merchant, Kumoch Park.[13] The article presented the discrepancies between the merchant's version of the shooting and character statements in support of the victim. The various statements by members of the local community leaned toward a view that the shooting was another act of disrespect, though there is not the videotape evidence present in LaTasha Harlins's case. The facts that Mitchell was unarmed, was not known by established members of the neighborhood, and had gone to the store on his bicycle were evidence given as statements of disbelief that the killing was justified.

Equally powerful was the visual contextualization of the Mitchell article. The headline of the article stood just below a graphic photograph of the open wounds of an African American man and a Latino man who were beaten by LAPD officers. The fact that the headline, "Black Man Killed by Korean Merchant: No Charges Filed," stood flush with the borders of the photograph of the police brutality victim created an illusionary association despite the fact that the two were entirely separate incidents.

A two-part series on the political machinations of a Korean grocer added a conspiratorial dimension to the archetype. The story is about a Korean merchant, James J. Oh, the owner of La Fiesta Food Warehouse and several other stores. The exposé-style article described how Oh lobbied and contributed campaign funds to five city councilpersons, who used city eminent domain power to acquire property that was then bought by Oh. He was also reported to be "guilty of threatening to fire employees and threatening to close down the store (Superior Warehouse) to discourage union activities."[14] In the second article, Reverend William R. Johnson, Jr., of Curry Temple C.M.E. church is quoted, "It's a shame that people like Oh come into our community making all this money and paying such low wages."[15] The article also notes that he has been picketed by community and labor organizations for reportedly paying half the going union wage, a wage that was ostensibly fought for by African Americans and others who had long been active in the local labor movement.

The portrayal of Koreans as collaborating with the power struc- ture became much more prominent with the unfolding of the trial and particularly with the absence of prison time in the sentence. In the second of a two-part interview with Judge Joyce Karlin, a question was asked by the *Sentinel* reporter, "How do you feel the Korean community perceives you now?" This was followed up with, "Not even the Korean Grocers Association? They stated in the *Korea Times* that they were raising money for your campaign." Karlin responded, "I don't think they see me as pro-Korean or anti-Korean."[16] The reporter's line of questioning suggests a po- litical motive on Karlin's part in issuing a lenient sentence to garner Korean support for her imminent reelection campaign and hints at collaboration on the part of members of the Korean community.

The consensus that the sentencing was "outrageous" was unan- imously voiced in the newspaper's articles, editorials, commentar- ies, and letters to the editor. The first editorial, under the title "An Outrageous Decision," referred to the sentence of the $500 fine and ten weeks of community service as "pitifully inadequate for the taking of the life of a teenage girl by shooting her in the back of the head while she was apparently moving away."[17] The editorial continued, "First it was the police. Now it is our judges who have become the messengers of this chilling edict: there is a different standard that is applied if you are a Black-suspect or victim, it doesn't matter."[18] Hence emerged the theme of unequal justice—or injustice. And in this case, Koreans took part in the infliction of injustice against African Americans.

A number of quoted statements and adjoining articles express similar outrage. Upon the one-year anniversary of Harlins's death, a member of the LaTasha Harlins Justice Committee was inter- viewed: "I'd like to say that Judge Karlin single-handedly did what 27 policemen did in the Rodney King case. . . . We also know that there is a dual standard in the judicial system when it comes to meting out sentencing for Black people."[19]

Lines of demarcation are drawn in the analysis of the sentencing of Soon Ja Du. A front page news analysis adjoining the coverage of the verdict stresses the unequal treatment by the justice system based on race:

Judicial decisions like those in both the Du case and the one in North Carolina point out that when it comes to the legal system, African American victims of violence perpetrated by Whites and others are exempt from the nation's "War on Crime."[20]

Koreans are placed in the category of "whites and others" who are not subject to the same treatment that African Americans are relegated. There is a boundary drawn along the lines of shared experience, with Koreans as "others" on the side of whites.

A stream of letters to the editor condemning the decision and also venting resentment toward Asians reinforces those boundaries with emotional charge. One letter, entitled "Respect Ourselves," categorized Asians together with the police department. The writer urged African Americans to respect each other or else "we will not be able to stop the disrespect from others and the continued racism from the police department, the Korean merchants, and other unconcerned races."[21]

In the four months following the verdict and sentencing, there were more letters published concerning unequal justice and Asians. Many of those, such as "What's Black Life Worth?" expressed outrage at the judge, stating that "my life to that judge means less than the feelings or even the life of a dog,"[22] in reference to the case of an African American imprisoned for beating a dog. Others, however, also expressed deep resentment toward Asians and revealed misconceptions of Koreans in America. An open letter to Judge Karlin incorrectly assumes that Koreans are not citizens or permanent residents of the United States and that they are protected by Korean law. The letter states: "It is ironic that a victim, with rights that were protected by the Constitution, was killed by a foreigner, and that the law of the victim's homeland protected the rights of her murderer more effectively than it demanded justice for the victim."[23] Another letter is written in protest of news that a Martin Luther King, Jr., Day poster features Koreans in the design. She writes that "this poster bespeaks what many Blacks fear is happening to them in Los Angeles: They are being pushed out of the picture. Immigrants are displacing Blacks economically and politically. And, according to the poster, our very presence is next."[24]

The resentment toward Asians expressed in the letters to the editor are tempered or challenged in other articles and editorials. There are clearly different viewpoints among the various contributing writers in their feelings toward Asian Americans. One editorial, entitled "Common Ground," stresses that African Americans, Koreans, and Latinos "all labor under the yoke of discrimination and bias, joblessness, inferior housing and a failure to vote in the numbers that we can" and called on community leaders and followers to "wake up and seek the common ground."[25]

Articles on the activities of the LaTasha Harlins Justice Committee and the selective buying campaign de-emphasized any resentment against Asians and instead emphasized community control by African Americans over the enterprises and institutions within their neighborhoods. Danny Bakewell defends the boycott of "merchants in South Central who are disrespectful to the African-American consumer." He explains the Brotherhood Crusade's efforts to acquire small businesses:

The reason we started this economic development push is that we can open up our own stores, sort of like a 7–11 chain. But we have to be about what we can do for ourselves and stop worrying about what other people may have.[26]

The reaffirmation of collective identity is partly cast in relation to actions in support of or opposition to movements concerning issues of justice. The voices of Bakewell, Denise Harlins, Brother David, and others working at the local community level are much more dominant in the frame than are African American elected officials. In fact, one article focuses on accusations against Mayor Tom Bradley for insensitivity to the Harlins family. Another article inferred a connection between Judge Karlin, Mayor Bradley, and other elected officials through a public relations firm, indirectly questioning those African American elected officials' commitment to the welfare of other African Americans. The efforts to appeal the sentence of Soon Ja Du, the campaign to recall Judge Karlin, and the selective buying campaign are highlighted as noble efforts.

It is very important to note, however, that even in the midst of the outrage after the sentence by Judge Karlin was handed down, an editorial in the *Sentinel*, entitled "An Outrageous Decision," began with a clarification of blame in the first paragraph: "Korean Americans are not to blame for what transpired in Superior Court last Friday; African Americans are not to blame for what happened last Friday. The judicial system is to blame."[27] Several other articles,[28] and a lengthy series on race relations, also warn of the dangers of rising ethnic conflict and call for mutual under-standing between ethnic groups.

It is clear from the contrast between the substance of the letters to the editor and the editorials themselves that the issue of blame and the question of strategy are controversial debates within the community. The irony, however, is that while the editorials attempted to stress common ground, cooperation, and nonviolent action, the cumulative weight of articles that portray Koreans as a negative influence in the African American com-munity seem to overpower editorial pleas against the scapegoat-ing of Koreans.

KOREA TIMES: CRIME, ETHNIC SCAPEGOATING, AND THE KOREAN AMERICAN DREAM

The framing of the events by the *Korea Times* tells a very differ-ent story. Just as LaTasha Harlins became a symbolic repre-sentative of the African American plight, so too did Soon Ja Du for the Korean immigrant to America. The focus of this frame con-cerns the tenuous relations between the Korean and African American communities and the potential impact of those relations on their realization of the American dream. Soon Ja Du's predica-ment is the story of the hardships faced by many Koreans who immigrated to the United States, surviving crime and scapegoat-ing in a historically African American neighborhood. The tension intensifies with announcements of the verdict and sentence, stir-ring the rage of many African Americans and resulting in more fear over hate crimes and racial attacks. The *Korea Times'* portrayal of the shooting of LaTasha Harlins considers not only the tragic death of an African American, but the equally unfortuitous eclipse of the American dream for Korean immigrants, personified by Soon Ja Du.

Many of the articles in the *Korea Times* strongly adopted the viewpoint of the Korean immigrant entrepreneur. This may be reflective of the high numbers and position of entrepreneurs within the community and their support for ethnic-based institu-tions, including the local media. But the articles also expressed a growing fear that backlash makes no class distinction. The anger of African Americans toward Korean merchants was seen to affect all Koreans and other Asian Americans. This further reinforced an ethnic and racial identity over a class identity in the symbolism of the case.

The conflicting interpretations of the shooting reported in the *Korea Times* immediately following the incident left room for uncertainty as to what transpired. An explanation by Soon Ja Du's son, Joseph, gave a lengthy account of what took place between Soon Ja Du and LaTasha Harlins as conveyed to him by his mother. He told of the scuffle between the two and an attempt by Harlins to steal money from the cash register. He was quoted, "But Harlins was undaunted and continued to hit Du. As she was about to faint from the blows, Du shot Harlins."[29] The release of a videotape of the incident later proved that this account was not true. The police account, which was also reported in that same issue of the *Korea Times*, offered a conflicting story that was consistent with the videotape that showed the scuffle ending with a shot being fired as Harlins was walking away from Soon Ja Du.[30] Added to the ambiguity was a subsequent headline story reporting a finding that the gun was faulty and was set to fire at the lightest touch of the trigger.[31]

In addition to these accounts, there were several articles that focused on character accounts of Soon Ja Du. One article, entitled "Mrs. Du: A Silent Helper of Lepers and Homeless,"[32] included testimony from her church minister. He described her as a "compassionate, faithful, God-fearing woman who was no criminal." She represented a fellow citizen driven to the edge in pursuit of the shared dream.

Placed against the backdrop of character accounts of Soon Ja Du, conflicting accounts of the incident, and the evidence of a faulty gun, the sentence did not necessarily appear unjust, as it had against the backdrop painted in the *Sentinel*. Two sets of interviews with community leaders and students were published in the *Korea Times* following the verdict. Of the over one dozen who expressed their views on the verdict, only two students tended to feel that the verdict was unfair and should have been harsher. In fact, greater than concern over the verdict itself was the concern over the response of the African American community. It was during this time that the thematic emphasis shifted to concern about the scapegoating of Koreans and the numbers of articles on anti-Asian and anti-Korean hate crimes rose.

What was omitted in the articles, but was mentioned in several interviews with local Korean American professors, was the racism and bigotry that an uncertain number of Korean immigrants held.[33] This type of issue is difficult to discuss in a public forum and would be viewed within the Korean American community as "airing dirty laundry." Nevertheless, there were both implicit and explicit acknowledgements of the problem of negative stereotyping of African Americans within the Korean American community.

The abundance of articles casting a very positive light on individuals from the African American community and spotlighting Koreans who have nurtured individual relationships with African Americans indirectly addresses the issue of racism among Korean Americans. It is a positive way of addressing a negative problem. In this way, the editorial staff appeared to make an effort to play a constructive role in mediating the conflict. K. W. Lee's nudging of the English-speaking *Korea Times* readership to practice good neighborliness is consistent with his stated belief that part of the problem is the practice or image of Koreans as uncaring for those in the neighborhood in which they do business.[34]

After the announcements of the verdict and sentence, there was an increase in the number of articles focused primarily on hate crimes and the activities of Ice Cube, a popular rap artist who released a controversial tune called "Black Korea." These articles included stories on hate crimes committed against Koreans and other Asians as well as attempts to stop the escalation of hate crimes. The articles on Ice Cube reported of the release of the *Death Certificate* compact disc and the controversy over the "Black Korea" and "No Vaseline" cuts. Quoting a portion of "Black Korea" including a stanza about burning a store in retribution for lack of "respect" to a black organization, the article ended with the mailing address to the president of the record company to which community leaders were urging people to write.[35]

The series of articles on Ice Cube told the story of a victory in the fight against Korean-bashing. Regular coverage appeared on the efforts of the Korean American Grocers Association to put a "freeze on Ice Cube."[36] They, along with other Korean grocers' organizations nationally, were reported to have pressured St. Ides

beer company to discontinue commercials and promotional materials that featured Ice Cube. As opposed to the form of mass
protest that the African American community used in its efforts
for justice, credit for the success of the campaign was attributed
to the unity and organization among Koreans to utilize the
weight of their economic position to change the behavior of
another business enterprise without government intervention.

The *Korea Times* editorial made it clear that a viable long-term
remedy to strained relations was the Korean community's commitment to be "good neighbors." This did not necessarily mean
a change in economic or power relationships, but the demonstra-
tion of benevolence toward African Americans. This remedy,
however, could just as easily lead to even greater resentment,
according to the frame of the *Sentinel*, which was more sympathetic to efforts to gain greater "community control" over economic institutions serving African Americans. The prescriptive
remedies as outlined in both frames can be viewed as offensive
and in opposition to the other. Patronage can simply be considered another form of disrespect; community control can mean the
expulsion of those outside of the boundary of an ethnically or
racially defined community.

ESCALATION AND SHIFTING FRAMES

In the case of both newspapers, the frames shifted in thematic
emphasis at the point at which the verdict was announced and the
judge handed down the sentence. The theme of the *Sentinel* frame
transitioned from "disrespect" to "injustice." The theme of "injustice" had greater resonance and power than that of "disrespect"
because it implied a structural problem, not simply an interper-
sonal one. It also suggested that conspiratorial, collusive, or systemic actions were consciously and irrevocably taken by those
involved. The simultaneous drama of the Rodney King case, in
which the theme of injustice was dominant from the beginning,
gave added power to the symbolism of the judge's sentence in the
Soon Ja Du case.

The fear of racial backlash to the verdict and sentence hastened
the transition in the frame of the *Korea Times* from "crime" to
"scapegoating." The fear of crime against merchants was general-
ized to fear of scapegoating against Koreans as an ethnic group

and Asians as a racial group. This minimized class distinctions since the threat of backlash was seen as devoid of class discrimination. In this case, Korean ethnic group identification was reinforced in response to the reaction of African Americans in their dealings with a select group of Korean Americans. Tensions escalated in response to an action of the judicial system, which was seen as serving justice unequally to African Americans. The blame placed on Koreans for the sentence led to fears of indiscriminate attacks against Koreans and Asian Americans. More groups become pulled into the controversy, which then began to gain its own momentum.

CONCLUSIONS

A study of the framing of events concerning the death of LaTasha Harlins and the trial of Soon Ja Du raises a number of policy and research implications. One concerns the material basis of conflict, the intractable nature of controversy, and alternative methods of reconciliation. Currently, a popular method of conflict resolution takes the form of dispute resolution. This method assumes that disagreements can be resolved through negotiation and compromise between contending parties. The fact, however, that the two frames indicate very different *definitions* of the problem makes dispute resolution techniques extremely difficult. Dispute resolution assumes that two parties can at least agree on the definition of the problem, which may be particularly difficult in situations of racial or ethnic conflict where historical experiences, socioeconomic status, cultural differences, language differences, and institutional networks may differ.

In this case study, the frames are steeped in the experiences of an immigrant's hardship, a young girl's death, a lenient sentence, different socioeconomic conditions, and distinct institutional structures within the Korean American and African American communities of Los Angeles. Dispute resolution cannot reverse, for example, the turn of events that prompted the escalation of tensions. Addressing the material and historic bases of conflict are fundamental to any long-term resolution of conflict.

Dispute resolution also does not address the problem inherent in "controversy." A useful distinction between "disagreements" and "controversies" has been made in discussions of policy discourse. Disagreements can usually be resolved by gaining access to information or negotiating compromises through such means as dispute resolution. Controversies, on the other hand, are much more difficult to resolve in a consensual way.[37] The incongruity of frames of the *Korea Times* and *Los Angeles Sentinel* points to an intractability of controversy. Further research on the role of ethnic media should not only reflect existing frames, but should construct frames that influence public interpretations of contemporary ethnic conflict and offer instructive insights.

Secondly, while economic inequity, political disfranchisement, disparate treatment within the justice system, and other problems are issues that must be addressed, the elimination of material inequities and reparation for past injustices would not, by themselves, eliminate the problem of ethnic conflict. The study of discordant frames suggests that the social realm of conflict must concurrently be addressed. The empowerment of people to work cooperatively to address material problems necessitates the expansion of frames to incorporate an understanding of the other. It is impossible for two different individuals or ethnic groups with different historical experiences to share the same frame. But the more understanding that each group can have of the "other" experience, the greater will be their ability to understand each other's problems as they are *self*-defined. It may be naive to think that one can rise above one's own experience, but the greater the level of mutual understanding, the better are the chances for reconciliation of one's problems in fuller consideration of *mutual* needs and interests.

Thirdly, the study of frames is useful in understanding how seemingly distinct issues may be connected. For example, there is evidence that some Korean-owned businesses in many areas of south Los Angeles and in Koreatown may have been selectively targeted in the uprising following the acquittal of the LAPD officers involved in the beating of Rodney King. Certainly, there were striking parallels between the two trials. Soon Ja Du shot LaTasha Harlins in the back of her head only two weeks after LAPD officers beat Rodney King. Both incidents were captured on videotapes which were then repeatedly aired on television broadcasts. Relations between the LAPD and the African American community as well as relations between many Korean merchants and south-central Los Angeles residents had been strained for some time. The two incidents were followed by related events. An African American man was shot by a different Korean merchant. A 9-year-old Korean American girl and several Korean grocers were shot and killed in separate robbery attempts, allegedly by African Americans. Concurrently, many more instances of police brutality were reported and publicized. There was also a change of venue in both trials to areas with much smaller percentages of African Americans. Though Soon Ja Du was convicted of involuntary manslaughter with the use of a gun, she received none of the up to sixteen years of imprisonment allowable in her sentence. LAPD officers were acquitted by the Simi Valley jury. Both the sentence and acquittal were considered by many as gross injustices against African Americans. Both incidents and initial trials took place within the fifteen-month period between March 1991 and May 1992, with the sentencing of Soon Ja Du taking place in November 1991.

There were also very important differences between the cases. Soon Ja Du was a Korean merchant of a mom-and-pop store. She was not a part of any state or police apparatus. The balance of power between the African American community and the police force is not comparable to the balance of power between the African American community and Korean merchants. Nor are members of the Korean community established in positions of political power equal to that of whites or African Americans in local government. The history of relations are also incomparable. Korean merchants have not had a history of abuse equivalent to that of the LAPD. Not that a body count can measure the tragedy that any group faces, but it is relevant to note that more Korean American grocers have been killed in robbery attempts by African Americans than African Americans killed by Korean merchants. Finally, the jury did not acquit Soon Ja Du, while the Simi Valley jury fully exonerated police officers of the major charges in the Rodney King trial.

There is evidence that part of the outrage at the LAPD officers' acquittal was expressed in anger toward Koreans and other Asian Americans. Spray-painted slogans captured in photos of the uprising stating "This is for LaTasha" point to this connection. It is my hunch that there is an overlay of issues that creates a "landmine" where an action on one issue may set off a chain reaction based on meanings and relationships placed upon those events by different groups of people. The study of frames may help us trace the logic of those connections. The framing in the *Sentinel* of both cases as "injustice," with the LAPD and Korean merchants as perpetrators of the injustice, place the police and Korean merchants in the same category. Thus, it is conceivable that the anger toward police in the aftermath of the LAPD officers' acquittal may have been directed, in part, toward Korean-owned businesses.

Just as conflict in one arena can escalate or trigger tension in another, the reverse can also be true. For example, Asian American participation in marches and rallies against police brutality can also affect the interethnic relations surrounding the LaTasha Harlins and Soon Ja Du case. Where there are links that can lead to the escalation of conflict, those same links can also lead to the building of cooperative relations. An understanding of the connections between issues may point to new opportunities for cooperation and to coalition efforts equipped to address larger social problems.

And finally, the primacy of the theme "injustice" raises further implications for theories of ethnic conflict in relation to states and public policy. Whether deliberate or unintentional, perceived or in fact, the unequal application of allegedly uniform public policy to groups differentiated along ethnic lines, especially to those ethnic groups without equal voice in the institutions of state power, can further divide society and exacerbate conflict between minority or subordinant groups. Not only do economic variables need to be analyzed, but ethnic or racial inequities in the state institutions—judicial, political, military, social, and cultural—need additional scrutiny and analysis.

Conservative policy reforms during the 1980s have weakened much of the civil rights legislation passed during the 1960s. The diminished role of the state in protecting civil rights and regulating the distribution of wealth and resources has exacted a toll on race relations. The legitimacy of the state and its institutions is fragile, as is evidenced by the most costly and volatile urban unrest in recent history. The civil unrest of April 1992 in Los Angeles after the Simi Valley jury's acquittal of the Los Angeles police officers in the Rodney King beating trial was not a race riot as much as a multiracial rebellion against the failure of a state institution—the judicial system. As state institutions fail to mediate equitable and just resolutions to the nation's economic, political, and social problems, individuals and groups have resorted to extralegal means of resolution. The continued failure of existing economic and political structures in bringing real and perceived equality and justice will certainly result in the weakening of the social contract and the escalation of conflict.

NOTES

1. Bureau of the Census, Current Population Survey (Washington, D.C., 1990).

2. Ibid.

3. Paul Ong, *The Widening Divide: Income Inequality and Poverty in Los Angeles* (Los Angeles: University of California at Los Angeles, 1989).

4. See also Mike Davis, *City of Quartz: Excavating the Future in Los Angeles* (New York: Verso, 1990), for a discussion on social and economic changes taking place in Los Angeles. For a review of studies on African Americans in the labor market, see also Philip Moss and Chris Tilly, *Why Black Men Are Doing Worse in Labor Market: A Review of Supply-Side and Demand-Side Explanations* (London: Sage Race Relations Abstracts, 1991).

5. Paul Ong et al., *Beyond Asian American Poverty: Community Economic Development Policies and Strategies* (Los Angeles: LEAP Asian Pacific American Public Policy Institute, 1994).

6. *Civil Rights Issues Facing Asian Americans in the 1990s: A Report of the United States Commission on Civil Rights* (Washington, D.C.: U.S. Commission on Civil Rights, February 1992). Also includes report on the rise in bigotry and violence against Asian Americans. See also Michael Thornton and Robert J. Taylor, "Intergroup Attitudes: Black American Perceptions of Asian Americans," *Racial and Ethnic Studies* 11 (November 1988), pp. 474–488.

7. See Edward Tea Chang, "New Urban Crisis: Korean-Black Conflicts in Los Angeles" (Ph.D. diss., University of California at Berkeley, 1990).

8. Bureau of the Census, 1987 Survey of Minority Owned Business Enterprises (Washington, D.C.).

9. Lucie Cheng and Yen Espiritu, "Korean Businesses in Black and Hispanic Neighborhoods: A Study of Intergroup Relations," *Sociological Perspectives*, vol. 32 (1989), pp. 521–534.

10. Marsha Mitchell, *Los Angeles Sentinel*, March 21, 1991.

11. "The Harlins Family: After the Tragedy and the Verdict," *Los Angeles Sentinel*, December 5, 1991.

12. Mitchell, op cit.

13. Marsha Mitchell, "Black Man Killed by Korean Merchant: No Charges Filed," *Los Angeles Sentinel*, June 13, 1991.

14. Dennis Schatzman, "Inner-City Grocer Knows Political Landscape," *Los Angeles Sentinel*, June 27, 1991.

15. Dennis Schatzman, "Controversy Follows Inner-City Grocer All Over L.A.," *Los Angeles Sentinel*, June 13, 1991.

16. "Interview," Judge Joyce Karlin, *Los Angeles Sentinel*, March 18, 1992.

17. "An Outrageous Decision," *Los Angeles Sentinel*, November 21, 1991.

18. Ibid.

19. "Anniversary: The Harlins Tragedy" (interview with the spokespersons for the LaTasha Harlins Justice Committee in rebuttal to the interview with Judge Karlin), *Los Angeles Sentinel*, March 25, 1992.

20. Dennis Schatzman, "Blacks and the Justice System," *Los Angeles Sentinel*, November 27, 1991.

21. Michel Baylor, "Respect Ourselves," *Los Angeles Sentinel*, April 24, 1991.

22. Herschel David Hunt, "What's Black Life Worth?" *Los Angeles Sentinel*, December 11, 1992.

23. Quinton D. Worthams, "Justice Not Equal," *Los Angeles Sentinel*, December 18, 1991.

24. Rita Green, "Asians and MLK Day," *Los Angeles Sentinel*, January 22, 1992.

25. "Common Ground," *Los Angeles Sentinel*, September 19, 1991.

26. "Bakewell Answers Critics," *Los Angeles Sentinel*, October 9, 1991.

27. "An Outrageous Decision," *Los Angeles Sentinel*, November 21, 1991.

28. The following articles appeared in the *Los Angeles Sentinel*: "Los Angeles: Ethnic Collision Course?" August 11, 1991; "Tensions Ignite: Critical Mass in Melting Pot," August 25, 1991; "The Melting Pot: Cooling Down a Flammable Mix," September 30, 1991.

29. Stephen W. Yum, "Soon Ja Du's Family Claims Self-defense," *Los Angeles Sentinel*, March 27, 1991.

30. "Police Say Dispute Led to Fatal Shooting: Grocer to Be Charged with First Degree Murder," *Korea Times*, March 27, 1991.

31. "Faulty Gun: Key to Du's Murder Trial," *Korea Times*, October 7, 1991.

32. "Mrs. Du: A Silent Helper of Lepers and Homeless," *Korea Times*, April 3, 1991.

33. K. W. Lee, "Fire Next Time? Edward Chang Reflects on the Black-Korean Conflict," *Korea Times*, June 2, 1991; K.W. Lee, "Fire Next Time:

Failure of Selfish Korean Elite," *Korea Times*, June 9, 1991; Sophia Kyung Kim, "KA Anthropologist: Many Views among Blacks" (interview with Kye Young Park), *Korea Times*, February 3, 1992.

34. A series of articles were run in the *Korea Times* that highlighted Korean merchants who exemplified "good neighbors."

35. "Chilling Fields: Ice Cube Rap," *Korea Times*, November 11, 1991.

36. Including "KAGRO Puts Freeze on Ice Cube," *Korea Times*, November 18, 1991.

37. See Don Shon and Martin Rein, *Reframing: Study of Policy Controversy* (unpublished manuscript, Winter 1992).

Part III

Lessons and Visions from the 1960s

8

Blacks and Chicanos: Parallels in Political and Historical Struggles

Daniel Osuna

Daniel Osuna is International Secretary of El Partido Nacional de La Raza Unida, a political party based in Phoenix, Arizona. The following is an excerpt of a presentation delivered by Mr. Osuna on February 22, 1993, at Michigan State University in East Lansing, Michigan. The occasion of this presentation was a conference sponsored by Michigan State University to explore and build bridges of communication between blacks and Latinos, on and off campus. This was the first such conference ever held in East Lansing, Michigan. Mr. Osuna was asked to make the keynote presentation based on his extensive experience of activism in the Chicano community, in addition to his work in building bridges between black and Latino activists in the 1960s.

I want to open by welcoming everyone. I suspect from what I've heard that this is the first black and Latino conference that has been held in this area to discuss the mutual understanding of both our people, and our situation, so that we can move forward collectively to change our conditions in the future. I'd like to extend on behalf of our organization, *revolutionary* greetings; and please don't get nervous about the use of this term. When you hear a commercial that says Revlon has just had a revolutionary new idea with hair spray, you don't get nervous, or another product says that they've had a revolutionary new idea that has taken them to a different place, you don't get nervous; when you hear that there's been a revolutionary breakthrough in medical science, you don't get nervous. As a matter of fact, you become happy! So, it is in a *revolutionary* spirit that we can rise above our situation in which we find ourselves and began to take ourselves to a higher plane of understanding.

I'd also like to extend on behalf of our organization, El Partido Nacional de La Raza Unida and the aspirations of our people, our unconditional and uncompromising support to the African community abroad and here in the United States.

Before I begin discussing the historical parallels of which this speech is entitled, there are a couple of points that were brought up in last night's and this afternoon's presentations that I'd like to address.

I would like to take issue with the statement about "sensitivity"; I've heard the statement about needing to be sensitive to other cultures. I know that Africans don't want me to be sensitive, I know they want my respect and that's what we want from all people. It's a question of respect, and ultimately power, and not one of sensitivity.

Also, in trying to deal with the question of identity, it's very difficult because I know about the challenges among some blacks. When you go to blacks who have been here for many generations and you say you're an African; some will say "I'm not an African, I'm not from Africa, I'm from here, I'm from America, I'm an American, I'm a black American." The same challenges go on in the Chicano or indigenous community of the western hemisphere. For too long Chicanos have not been seen as Indians, and Northern Native American Indians may sometimes disclaim the fact that Chicanos could possibly be Indian or even Native American.

I'd like to give an explanation for America because anyone born in the continent of America, whether it be from the tip of Chile or Alaska, is an American. We cannot allow a small group of people in Northern territories to control that term and say that it belongs to them solely. So when I speak of Americans, I am speaking of the people of the Americas and primarily the indigenous people of the Americas, and when I speak of Africa, I will speak of those indigenous people of Africa.

There was one other point that I thought was real important that I felt I needed to clarify, and I say this with all due respect. Some of us have defined, or described, ourselves as "mixed blood." How many Africans know for a fact there's white blood in their lineage, but you don't see them calling themselves "of mixed blood" or calling themselves anything other than African or African American. When you go to a Native American and his father is white or his mother is white, you don't see him or her using any term except "Native American." Why is it we always feel as Mexicanos or Chicanos that we have to pay an allegiance to Spain or Europe?*

I am not a "Hispanic"! I am a Chicano Yawkee. Chicano is the root word, which comes from Mexicano, the people of which were originally known as the Aztecs. The Mexicans referred to themselves as Mexicanos.

Last year, on October 12th in San Francisco, one of the major celebrations of the five hundredth anniversary of the landing of Columbus was held, and there were three representatives that got up to speak; one native Northern American, one Mexicano, and one African. The Native American got up and started to talk about his indigenous roots and his lineage, including the long history of Native American people in the United States. He also talked about and bragged about how far their people had been connected to all other Indians and all other peoples, and all groups needed to heed that fact. The Mexican representative got up and started saying that Mexicanos were Indians and some of those Indians had been here longer than the Northern Native Americans, and then the African got up and started to say, well all of you are crazy, we all came from Africa, we all need to pay homage to Mother Africa.

---

* As explained some time ago by David Hayes-Bautista, "The terms currently in vogue—'Hispanic' and 'Spanish origin'—are both misleading, stereotypical, and racist. Spain is a European country and its inhabitants are white people of European stock. No Spaniard has ever suffered undue discrimination, either in Latin America or in the United States. Raza, be they Chicanos, Mexicanos, Puerto Ricans, etc., have not been denied access to social benefits because they might have had a distant Spanish ancestor; discrimination has been suffered because raza are of Indian descent. . . . Continued use of the terms 'Hispanic' or 'Spanish origin' denies the very basis upon which discrimination has been based, and confuses the basis for civil rights and affirmative action efforts."

It is in those types of statements of people that our so-called leaders say they're speaking on our behalf, but yet are emulating their oppressor in every action and in every statement by narrowing the scope of where we're trying to go as human beings. This is useful to these so-called leaders to protect their own little egotistical world of what they're trying to develop with their own small power base. This is exactly why it is so important for people of color to understand our histories and how such are connected to each other, and in fact, parallel each other—and why!

Let me point out, that as important as are historical parallels between blacks and Chicanos for reigniting a racial movement for the future, this is certainly not enough. But while we can't stop at the historical parallels of our two peoples, we must start here. If we don't start from the reference point of our historical origins and parallels in order to understand and analyze our joint victimization, as well as our joint victories, then we cannot develop the correct solution to oppressions that we all face and must confront.

Young people, both African and Chicano, have yet to understand their place among humanity and how it parallels other peoples of color in this planet. From the pyramids in Egypt, to the pyramids in the Americas, we reflected similar structural and economic conditions and gave support through struggle to similar cultural values.

When Vasco da Gama was landing in Africa, Christopher Columbus was landing in America. When the African ancestry was sold into slavery, what do you think was happening in the Americas? The indigenous people of America were being sold to slavery at the same time—and by the same people. When the Mandinka and the Fulani tribes were resisting against the European invasions, the Inca and the Mashika tribes were resisting against the European invasions. When Shaka Zulu (not the one you saw on the TV movie) was planning and leading one of the most valiant resistances to colonialism in Africa, a young man of seventeen, Cuahtemoc, was leading the resistance of the "Mexico" (pronounced me-she-ka) empire, one of the greatest empires in the Americas, in what you know as Mexico today.

In the 1800s when indigenous people of Africa were leading revolts on a mass scale all over Africa against European invasions by the British, against the French, against the Dutch, then so were the indigenous people of the Americas from North America to

South America leading against the French, against the Dutch, against the British. Always at the same time, sometimes simultaneously, but not always in the same place; we were fighting against the same enemy continuously throughout our respective histories!

In 1831, when Nat Turner led one of the most valiant slavery revolts in the United States, it was in 1848, just a few years later, that a wonderful human being named Juan Neopmuceno (Cheno) Cortina, the founder of the organization that I represent, was leading one of the mass revolts of the takeover the southwestern United States. Simultaneously, sometimes, even at the same time, but always against the same enemy.

When there were mass lynchings of Chicano, Mexicanos, and other indigenous people such as the Navaho and Apache, in the Southwest, at the same time, and simultaneously, blacks were being lynched in the United States. In the "black belt" of the United States the Ku Klux Klan wreaked havoc and violence on the lives of blacks—but the KKK (we call them "Texas Rangers" in Texas) was also attempting to murder and control our people in the Southwest.

When W.E.B. Du Bois and Marcus Garvey were taking the lead in beginning the talk of the Pan Africanism, people like Bert Corona and Emma Tenayuca in the southwest and other parts of the Americas were taking the lead to change conditions for Chicano Mexicanos in the United States.

It is interesting and significant that when the spirit of Pan Africanism was being lead by Kwame Nkrumah in Africa, in Ghana, that in Central America and South America the spirit of Pan Americanism was on the discussion table regarding how to unify the indigenous forces of Chile, all the way up to Alaska. When the Student Non-Violent Coordinating Committee (SNCC) emerged in the United States, Latino GIs were also forming defense committees in the southwest in the United States.

When we go and talk to African students, some invariably say, "you can't possibly understand, we can't work together because you can't possibly understand what its like to be a slave." And, I ask these young students, were you ever a slave? Do you understand what it's like to be a slave? The answer is no. It is this kind of artificial barrier, however, despite our good intentions, that from our ignorance and not understanding the parallels of our history, we make statements that continue to keep us apart, instead of bringing us together as a people.

When I go to young Chicanos, sometimes they say, I don't want to work with black people; they got an attitude; they don't know what it's like; I mean you know, they haven't had their land taken away from them; so what, if they've been slaves. Again, reflecting ignorance of their own culture and history, they make statements that keep us further apart, instead of bringing us together.

But remember, students learn by example, and youth learns by example, and what we are setting as we participate in this conference is a theme and action plan for bringing us together. This kind of conference is long overdue, and it is the first time that we here in Lansing have talked about black and Latino unity, and how, in fact, the history of African and Chicano peoples represent continuity along parallel lines.

wider context

When Malcolm X and Martin Luther King were leading the pathway, there were people like Vernon Belacourt and Rodolfo (Corky) Gonzalez who were leading the way for Chicano Mexicanos and other indigenous people in the southwest, and in Mexico, and throughout the western hemisphere.

You may not know who those people are, media attention may not have captured or reported them to you, but their voices in their community were just as great as the voice of Malcolm X. In their communities, their voices of freedom and social change were just as great as the voice of Martin Luther King.

When the Black Panthers were on the rise, in Oakland and Chicago the organization that I represent, La Raza, existed in over thirty states in the East Coast, Midwest, and Southwest at the same time, simultaneously. We even strategized with the Black Panthers over security; they assisted us, and we assisted them on many occasions.

Why don't we know, or act upon, these historical connections and parallels? Our enemy can choose and the media can choose who they want to take into the limelight at any time that they choose, based on ignorance of our parallel cultures and history.

We have *both* fought the British, we have *both* fought the French, we have *both* fought the Dutch, we have *both* fought the Spanish, the Portuguese and even the so-called Americans, we have *both* fought them and still fight them today in the pursuit of racial equality and racial justice. Understand this, this is the history that is true, and that ultimately counts for us as two oppressed peoples!

In our communities today, it is we, blacks and Chicanos, who suffer from social, economic, and educational problems across the board, simultaneously, at the same time and always, always, always by the same system. We must, therefore, move forward together, or not at all.

Linda Chavez, a so-called leader of the "Hispanic Community" (and that's probably where she belongs), argues for assimilation in her book entitled *On the New Road to Hispanic Assimilation*. I have something to share with you brothers and sisters, both black and Latino: Assimilation is not freedom.

As a people of color we have much to offer, and continue contributing to humanity. I made this claim in 1978 as a student organizer. I never understood the depth of that statement. I made it, probably heard it from one of my mentors at one time, but I never understood it to the depth of which I understand it now. As I said then, Western European cultures have never understood their place among humanity.

Today, psychologists and sociologists are beginning to point out that we need to learn to act on the basis of a strong cultural foundation in order to develop confidence and self-esteem. It is not just about being independent but is about rising above and becoming independent so that we can work together as human beings to change and move together and advance humanity. We cannot do this, however, if we denigrate our cultures and disrespect each other's culture.

Supremacists arguing for the greatness of Western European cultures argue that this culture escaped the dark ages a long time ago—No, no, no, no. Western European cultures are barely at a point in recognizing, even at an intellectual level, that it is truly the interaction with all cultures, in their fullest development, that can take humanity where we need to go. Not any one culture or nation has a monopoly on enlightenment. And advanced technology does not necessarily guarantee enlightenment. Were not the Nazis technologically advanced during the 1930s and 1940s? Too many times, we've made the mistake of assuming that technology guarantees enlightenment. We can send a man or woman to the moon, but we can't even get along in our own communities.

Two years ago, our organization decided to sponsor the first joint Chicano/Americano indigenous North American Indian and African Youth Conference in the Denver area as a pilot program.

They told us it can't be done, they won't get along; you will have gang problems between blacks and Latinos, it can't be done; the Denver public school system would not support us, most of the civic and government organizations would not support us; only a handful of grassroots people came forward to support the planning and holding of this kind of conference.

Despite the naysayers, we had over five hundred youth that came out on their spring break to an all-day conference to hear about their culture and history and how young people could help bring together, for progressive activities, indigenous people in America, with the indigenous people from Africa, in order to change their joint social and economic conditions.

Don't tell me it can't be done. Blacks and Chicanos can come together in order to change their similar oppressions. When we stop allowing those other people to lead us, to make us believe that assimilating is the way out, progressive people of color will come together and represent a powerful force for social change in this nation.

One final point: Don't believe that you simply have to get rid of all the Western Europeans in this country in order for you to come together. Do you think you'd be better off; you think gang violence would stop if Western Europeans were to go? You think the division among our people would stop? No. The only strategy that guarantees this, is people joining together to create a socially just society for all. When communities of color come together to change the system for the benefit of all people, then social justice for everyone will prevail in the United States.

9

The Impact of Malcolm X on Asian-American Politics and Activism

Yuri Kochiyama

The following interview with Yuri Kochiyama was conducted on May 19, 1972, by Miya Iwataki for radio station KPFK in Los Angeles as part of a celebration of Malcolm X's birthday. It was slightly revised and updated by Ms. Kochiyama in June 1993. This interview and Yuri Kochiyama's concluding statement not only summarize how Malcolm X's thinking and actions influenced the Asian community in the United States, but thereby suggest at least one basis for political collaboration between black and Asian activists. Ms. Kochiyama has a long history of activities in the United States and abroad. In addition to being a close friend of Malcolm X, she has also worked extensively in the Asian community. A concluding statement by Yuri Kochiyama reflects the impact of Malcolm X on her recent activities.

THE INTERVIEW (1972)

Q: Now Yuri, when did you and your family first move to Harlem?

Kochiyama: We moved in December of 1960.

Q: What made you decide to live in Harlem?

Kochiyama: We were looking for a larger apartment. We were living in another project more in midtown in Amsterdam Houses and this new project Manhattanville was just going up. Luckily my husband happened to be working in that area and anyone who lived in that proximity had priority.

Q: And how did you first meet Malcolm X?

Kochiyama: It was quite a while ago. It was nine years ago on October 16, 1963, to be exact; it was in the foyer of the Brooklyn criminal court. Malcolm had come to follow up on the aftermath of some 600 people who were arrested in the summer of 1963 demonstrations at Down State Medical Center site in Brooklyn which was a fight for construction jobs for blacks and Puerto Ricans. He was still in the Nation of Islam so he could not or did not participate but he was always wherever his people were. He had no bodyguards, he was just by himself and he was immediately surrounded by admiring young blacks, mostly people from Brooklyn CORE. Seeing all the black people rush toward him, naturally I wanted to meet him too, although I wasn't sure he would talk to a nonblack. But I did go over there eventually and I was just overwhelmed by his charisma and his warmth.

Q: How did he respond to you as a Japanese American woman?

Kochiyama: He was just a very, very warm human being and I don't think the nationality mattered, even though at that time everyone was saying that he does not respond to whites, but I think that there are many whites who knew him quite well and who he respected and who respected him. He used to speak at the Socialist Workers Party Forum.

Q: Yuri, having lived and worked with Malcolm in Harlem, can you describe those times? What was Harlem like then and what was the black liberation movement like then? And what changes did you see taking place after Malcolm started working with the sisters and brothers there?

Kochiyama: The first question . . . I lived in Harlem yes, but of course I didn't "work" with Malcolm. He was a nationally recognized black leader and I was just a newcomer to the movement. I didn't know "nothing about nothing." We were in totally different "ball games," as I said I was just a neophyte in the civil rights movement that was for integration and he was an integral part of the black liberation movement . . . that's totally different. He was a nationalist, more correctly a "revolutionary nationalist." So you could see there was a tremendous difference.

Now, the question about what was the black liberation movement like, I don't think there was a clear definition of the black liberation movement then. I think it was almost everything from the post-Garvey nationalism to a struggle for democratic rights and against racism. But when Malcolm spoke of nationalism he meant black nationhood . . . totally free from white America. He meant a land base, he meant sovereignty, and he always spoke about self-determination, self-reliance, and self-defense.

Q: Well, what kind of impact did you feel that Malcolm and his teachings had on the Harlem that you lived in and knew?

Kochiyama: Well, I think that because there were many different kinds of movements, I think that most important is the impact he made about the awareness of . . . knowing oneself . . . and to know one's history, one's heritage. And then, to link it with politics. [This is where the] . . . black consciousness movement and black power movement followed along with the Black Panther party and the Republic of New Africa were born. Many people are not aware that these were actually two different Black Panther parties in Harlem.

Q: Did you . . . Were you able to view his organizing skills and how people in Harlem responded to his strength and his teaching and his visions of black people and what they should and could become?

Kochiyama: Well, I think you have to remember that Malcolm was way ahead of most of the people. So, no matter what organizing skills that he had, he had a lot of things to go up against . . . obstacles. Let's put it this way, Harlem was a nationalist's enclave but the civil rights movement was fast growing in the 1960s and the civil rights movement was integrationist and it was countering the nationalism. The media was antinationalist and did a scorching job on Malcolm; it depicted him a fanatic, a mad man, a hater, so, he had that to fight against too. I cannot say that all of his skills were utilized in the way that he would have liked to have done.

Q: Were the people afraid of him because of how the media portrayed him? Or did they gradually come to embrace the ideas?

Kochiyama: Oh, I think he had tremendous following . . . but he was not really an independent person at that time because he was still under Elijah Muhammad and I think he was constantly changing and he was growing above and beyond his "father" (meaning Elijah). He was growing beyond him in his knowledge and his understanding of what was happening in the world, especially in Africa . . . and I think the people definitely were seeing that what Malcolm was saying held a lot more water. . . .

Q: What are some of the experiences or incidents that are still living strongly in your memory of Malcolm?

Kochiyama: Well, we just mentioned what a difficult time Malcolm had with the press and the power structure attacking him all the time. I would say that what I remember about him . . . is the tremendous courage it must have taken to be able to say all the things that he did when no one else was saying them. He was condemning American hypocrisy and American duplicity, its illusions and misconceptions. And even though he got the full blast of the media's assault, he never backed off. He stood firm. I would also add that in dealing with the power structure he was intransigent, when it came to principles; but he was flexible with his own people, when it came to tactics.

Q: Is there a specific incident or experience that you remember happening that you can just tell us here in Los Angeles because many of us weren't able to be in a city where Malcolm was? Just an event that you can remember that had quite a large impact on yourself or the community that you lived in.

Kochiyama: The time that he came to our apartment when we were having a reception for the Hiroshima-Nagasaki World Peace Study Mission for writers. It was to be held on June 6, 1964, and, of course, that date would be just a few months after he bolted from the Nation of Islam. Most people told us, oh Malcolm would never come. Why would he go to a strange place and to an Asian home? But he did come.

Q: These were four writers from Japan?

Kochiyama: Three writers, all Hibakushas, atom bomb victims. When he knocked and we opened the door and saw him, we were all so excited—we could hardly believe it. Our place was jampacked from the living room, kitchen, all the way to the back bedrooms, and in the hallway, with civil rights activists as well as the three writers and some other Japanese Hibakushas. The house was full of Harlem-recognized civil rights leaders; white civil rights activists, and some Japanese that we asked to be host and hostesses.

He said he was quite amazed to see so many people there and he said he would like to meet everyone. So, he went through parts of the house shaking hands with everyone. It was one-third black, one-third white and, well, maybe not quite one-third Asian, but his warmth just amazed everyone, and it was really just overwhelming, and everybody was quite excited about him. The Hibakushas asked that the translators not interfere once Malcolm got started. He told the group a little bit about his prison life and that that's where he did most of his studying. He described the course of Chinese history and Japanese history and offered the difference that China, like most all Asian countries, went through feudalism and foreign domination, but that Japan was the only Asian country that was not transgressed upon in order to be occupied. It went straight from feudalism to capitalism; thus Japan was intact and strong until she was defeated in World War II. I think people were quite surprised at all the things that he said, and then he spoke of Vietnam.

Q: Well, what was Malcolm's knowledge of other people internationally . . . like the Asian people and other third world people?

Kochiyama: Malcolm said, "the struggle of Vietnam is the struggle of all third-world people," capsulizing that Asian and third-world people's fight was against foreign domination, imperialism, and colonialism. He had great admiration for Mao and Ho Chi Minh. Malcolm was so well-read already about Asian and third-world people's struggles, his knowledge and perspective was very keen and astute.

Q: What kind of effect did you see or feel that Malcolm had on third world people both here in America and internationally?

Kochiyama: As for third-world people or people of color here, he's constantly and continuously being quoted in movement newspapers, and by black, radical leaders, and leftist activists. He's definitely an inspiration to the movement here. As for the black struggle itself, he's unquestionably the guiding light, a very key example. . . . He is the source for political clarity. The provisional government of the Republic of New Africa was established on the concepts of Malcolm's thoughts and I think that's a great tribute to have a nation derived out of this man's life. Internationally, despite the character assassination that the American press did on him, he was admired in revolutionary circles worldwide. They understood him. I just want to cite some particularities. A Uruguayan Christian minister wrote a play about Malcolm, which was performed in Uruguay in 1966; in Chile in 1967; Cuba in 1969; in Czechoslovakia in 1970; and Poland in 1971. Malcolm is on a stamp in Iran. Malcolm's life has been written in Italian, French, German, Spanish, and Japanese. He is highly esteemed in all the progressive African countries; Arab countries too. The Chinese ambassador to Ghana was so impressed by Malcolm that he held a special banquet for him.

That day when Malcolm came to that reception for the Hibakushas, a black teacher from the Harlem Freedom School read a two-page typewritten letter by [Ghanaian] students who wrote glowingly of Malcolm's impact on the students of Ghana. He had just been to Ghana and had spoken with them. Also, of course, we all know that Malcolm made trips to the Arab world and Africa and he made contacts with many heads of states and also made the pilgrimage to Mecca. Wherever he spoke, he spoke of the black struggle in America; so he internationalized it. He also spoke at one of the OAU (Organization of African Unity) conferences in Tanzania. He brought together Africans from the two continents, from the mother-land and those here and in the diaspora, and he linked the struggles as one.

Q: What kind of impact did Malcolm's life and teachings have on the Asian American movement as you saw it? And you've mentioned many examples, but if there are any more examples of the impact that Malcolm had on Asians internationally.

Kochiyama: Well, you know Malcolm always stressed things like, if you don't know who you are and where you come from, meaning your heritage and history, how can you know in which direction to go? I feel that the Asian American movement heeded his words because through Asian American studies people delved into history to learn of the past, to learn about feudalism in Asia, of foreign domination and then here in America, about colonized mentality, being assimilated and of being a "banana"—yellow on the outside and white on the inside—like oreo cookies for blacks and pinto beans for the browns and Indians—I think Asians felt we had to find ourselves and feel pride in our Asian-ness.

Q: Can I just jump in here for a second? I think that . . . for myself I was a little before the time that they had Asian studies and so for myself and a lot of friends that I had I think one of the really important impacts that Malcolm had on us is that in Los Angeles, in particular, there are a lot of Asian street people . . . ex-felons, ex-addicts that were not accepted in our community during the 1960s. (And) I think through the teachings of Malcolm and what we saw, the kind of work we saw he was able to do, in the black community, gave us inspiration to start drug abuse programs like Asian American Hard Core where ex-addicts and ex-felons worked with addicts and felons and helped work out, things around identity, why were they turning to drugs in the first place. Why did they have to steal, rip off their own people. A lot of these brothers and sisters did not like to read, but when we had readings like the *Autobiography of Malcolm X*, or even the sets of albums that have all his speeches, that really had a tremendous impact in winning them over into the movement and they're still here today.

Kochiyama: That's wonderful. Well, I certainly think he did the same thing here in the black community because you know . . . there are always those who are never included into the mainstream . . . even within the third-world communities there are people on the periphery. (And) I think Malcolm reached those people. He cleaned up, especially, those on drugs; no social workers could have done anything like that.

Q: What similarities do you see in the struggle of New African Freedom Fighters and the Asian Pacific American people? I mean . . . what areas of unity do you feel that our movements have?

Kochiyama: Well, the commonality of the two people I think would be in the commonality of the suffering. By suffering I mean the racism in this country; that all people of color in this country have had many similar experiences; for example, recently the Japanese Americans have been organizing a redress reparation movement because of their internment camp experiences. It happens to all third-world people, only they give it a different name. Africans were put on plantations. They were concentration camps. The American Indians were put in reservations, which were concentration camps. Wherever there is a concentration of people who have been dispossessed and disempowered, they are in concentration camps, and although it is not the same as what the Jewish people went through in Europe because they were in "death camps," all third-world people have gone through a similar kind of experience here. The Chinese, while they were building the railroads, lived in railroad camps that were very much like concentration camps. I think that the Chicano migratory workers camps were like concentration camps.

Q: You know a lot of us feel that you were so fortunate to be able to even meet him . . . right?

Kochiyama: Oh my goodness, yes!

Q: And just what kind of impact or effect did he have on you and how did you find him as a person, and as a friend, because many of us just know him from media or his writings; what was the human side of him?

Kochiyama: He certainly changed my life. Well, I know it might sound a little bit corny, but I feel that Malcolm's impact on my life was like that biblical story of Paul being struck by a light on the Damacus road; I feel that it happened to me. As I said, I was heading in one direction, integration, and he was going in another, total liberation, and he opened my eyes. He opened my mind, like opening a door to a new world. He helped me to start thinking, studying, listening, and observing and seeing contradictions. As a friend and as a person I felt he was a very humble person, very patient, he was very open, he was kind. He had great depth and breadth, there was nothing petty about him. He was just a . . . a phenomena. Everyone who's met him has said that he did change their life.

When I first met him I had the gall to tell him that I disagreed with his feelings on integration. He didn't look at me with scorn or ridicule, he was a very big person. He just smiled and said well, let's discuss it: we can't discuss it here, on the floor, you know, in the courthouse. He just said, come to my office. Of course that never did take place because he was busy traveling all the time, but he asked me to start attending his OAU meetings, enrolling in his liberation school, which I did; I feel that through the course of going to these meetings, and the school, that it helped me to understand what Malcolm was trying to say.

Q: When you met and spoke with Malcolm and attended the liberation school, did that change your views on integration and assimilation to total liberation?

Kochiyama: Oh, definitely! It was just an eye opener. Malcolm was too busy to teach in his Malcolm X liberation school. A man by the name of Jim Campbell handled the classes; also there was a teacher from East Africa and it was unlike any school I have ever attended. Although, prior to that, I and my whole family participated in the Harlem Freedom School, which only taught about Afro-American history; but Malcolm's school went beyond that because it linked us so closely with Africa, and of course they didn't see the struggle as a civil rights movement; they saw it as a "human rights" movement.

Q: What involved you . . . what made you get involved in such an integral role . . . you and your whole family with the black movement?

Kochiyama: I guess we were just lucky that we moved up to Harlem in 1960. Although we lived in a low-income project before that, and by the end of the twelve years that we were there it was mostly black and Puerto Rican—although it began exactly opposite, 60 percent white and 40 percent black and Puerto Rican.

There was a difference, I think, when we got up to Harlem. Harlem is definitely a nationalist enclave and you can't help but feel it. I think we were lucky, too, that we got to meet so many people that sort of pulled us into the movement. Where we lived Sonia Sanchez lived in the next building; Bill Epton was in another building in the project here; and we even heard that Paul Robeson, himself, was living in these projects because his son lived there. It was just, sort of natural living in this community to also become a part of it.

Q: Yuri, have you been attacked or harassed in any way because of your beliefs and your closeness with Malcolm and other revolutionary nationalist struggles?

Kochiyama: Not any more than anyone else, but I have to be careful because I think from reading my files that where it said . . .

Q: Which files are these?

Kochiyama: I got my Freedom of Information Act files and it showed that they were watching me just to see what contacts I made. So I would have to be very careful not to bring heat on certain activists in the black liberation movement.

Q: As we stated earlier in your introduction, you were present at the time of his assassination and what are your memories of that terrible day?

Kochiyama: Yes, that day was February 21st, on a Sunday . . . Sunday afternoon. My sixteen-year-old son Billy and I went to the Audubon, and as soon as we entered the hall we felt that there was a sort of an eerie feeling that something was going to happen. Well, also, I guess, because we heard that Malcolm was uptight when he came in earlier, and we also heard that all the invited speakers backed off and declined or canceled that day, and only brother Benjamin was going to be up on the stage. Well, then Benjamin said a few words, and strangely he did say something to the effect that Malcolm is the kind of man who'd be willing to die for you. Shortly after that Malcolm came on and he only got to say a few words beyond "A Salaam Alaikum" and everyone responded to him, when a ruckus in the middle section of the hall began.

We were sitting right across about the tenth or eleventh row facing the podium and was right in the center section across from us, when a man jumped up and said, "Get your hands out of my pocket," then after that, it seemed like all hell broke loose. Two or three men rose up from the front and they started shooting and the whole place went into utter chaos. Brothers were chasing those who did the shooting. Chairs were crashing to the floor, people were hitting the floor; there was screaming. A brother in front of me ran to the platform so I followed after him. We found Malcolm had fallen backwards on the stage and we were shocked to see how many times he was hit. He was having difficulty breathing; I don't think he even got to say a word and then he lost consciousness. In the meantime, people were running, screaming, running all over and people were trying to call the Presbyterian Hospital, which was only across the street. They were waiting for medical help and it seemed like it was forever before the medical people came with a stretcher. The shock, the grief, the anxieties, just engulfed everyone. We didn't know that . . . well we didn't know whether Malcolm was still alive. We didn't know if he was beyond help. Sister Betty (Shabazz) was very brave trying to keep the children as calm as possible.

Anyone who was there would never forget this date. I think it was a turning point in the black struggle. I felt it reinforced that there was a hidden war against blacks who dared to rebel; people like Malcolm who dared to go another way, who dared to be independent. I think it brought to light all the things that Malcolm was saying . . . That this country will let certain people survive here, but this country just wanted you to become puppets, robots, clowns, and pets, but for any black man or woman who stood up to them, that person would be in trouble.

Malcolm's assassination, I feel, was inevitable. The FBI and CIA were close on his heels. There were many indications, like when he was poisoned in Egypt the summer before his death; also, before he went to Africa, the U.S. government sent memos there to different African governments to discredit him; they even used African Americans.

Malcolm was just becoming too powerful and too many people were listening to him and he became a threat to this government. They just had to shoot him. Well, I'd like to maybe just end this with an analogy; the analogy is that he was like a strong tree that protected and inspired his people; because of that the enemy cut it down. But they only cut the trunk of the tree. The roots will always continue to grow and the seeds of Malcolm, and by seeds I mean his ideas, that they're everywhere and they're growing in the fertile minds of young black "Bloods," and the future generation of new Africans in America will continue to fight the struggle that he could not see through to the end . . .

Q: I want to thank you very much Yuri for your input in our program celebrating the birthday of Malcolm X, a great teacher and leader, of not only the black people in America, but all third-world people.

MALCOLM X: DOES HIS MESSAGE HAVE
RELEVANCE TO ASIAN AMERICANS TODAY?

Malcolm's life and what he did with it, rising from the muck of enforced poverty to international recognition, is primarily a message to his own people—black people in America, Africa, and the diaspora. But the significance of his feat in transforming his life, makes him relevant to all humanity. His life is truly a lesson to prove that one can transcend adversity, hate, and lies. Through struggle, he became the symbol of fearlessness against powerful enemies, of commitment to fight racism in this society, and a motivator to seek truth. Thus, his life and his message certainly should have relevance to Asian Americans.

Spike Lee's "Malcolm X" may be resurrecting him to a wider audience, but those who loved and followed Malcolm throughout the 1950s and 1960s to the moment of his assassination have devotedly given him the allegiance and esteem through these twenty-seven years without fanfare and publicity. There never has been a February 21, his assassination date, that there has not been countless commemorations in the black communities. There has never been a May 19, his birthday, that there was not a pilgrimage to his grave site.

Around the world, people and nations have honored him. Malcolm's picture appears on the postage stamp of Iran. Plays about him have been performed in Uruguay, Chile, Cuba, Poland, and Czechoslovakia. His writings have been translated into Italian, Spanish, German, French, Japanese, and African languages. In the last year of his life, he was invited to the African Summit Conference in Cairo, to a Conference of the Organization of African Unity, and the Commonwealth Ministers Conference in London. He also made the long-awaited sacred pilgrimage to Mecca in Saudi Arabia.

When Malcolm was killed at the Audubon Ballroom in Harlem, there was a Japanese writer and his wife who witnessed the assassination. The journalist, who uses the pen name Ei Nagata, had been to many Malcolm rallies. He wrote the first stories of Malcolm's death for Japanese newspapers. Malcolm was not a stranger to Asian history. During his seven years in prison, he read everything he could get his hands on. He loved reading history, history of every part of the world, even though the material on world history was Eurocentric.

In June 1964, Malcolm came to our apartment to meet with some Hibakusha writers of the Hiroshima/Nagasaki World Peace Study Mission, as these Japanese wanted to meet Malcolm more than any other figure in America. At that time, Malcolm's life was in danger as he had bolted from the Nation of Islam only a few months earlier. No one really expected Malcolm to show, but a large number of civil rights activists, both black and white, paced our apartment, perhaps out of curiosity. None were actual Malcolm people. There were no Muslims, Yorubas, nationalists, or radicals. The mixed group who came were, however, community activists. They perhaps wondered if Malcolm would be cold, critical, and intimidating. To everyone's surprise, they found Malcolm warm, gracious, open, and sensitive.

On learning that the Hibakushas had just gone to the world's "worst fair" in Harlem, Malcolm thanked them for choosing to come to the real-life fair, rather than the well-publicized, commercial World's Fair in Flushing Meadow. The Hibakushas saw what life in some parts of Harlem is like: garbage piled up because the city was not picking it up regularly; windows and stairwells broken and unrepaired; toilets that would not flush; bathtubs that were clogged. He said something to the effect: "You were bombed and have physical scars. We also have been bombed and you saw some of the scars in our neighborhood. We are constantly hit by the bombs of racism—which are just as devastating."

He spoke of Asia as a continent in which most of the countries have been colonized, and thus have had their sovereignty weakened. Only Japan, he said, had not been transgressed upon until the recent World War II when it was vanquished by the United States. But because it had not been colonized earlier, he explained, it was able to stay intact and strong. However, I do not think Malcolm was aware of Japan's similarity to America in its racism and chauvinism that inflicted irreparable damage to neighboring nations—especially South Korea.

He spoke highly of Mao Tse Tung, as he felt Mao had moved in the right direction to simultaneously fight feudalism, corruption in the hierarchy, and foreign domination. He liked Mao's selection of giving preferential treatment to the peasants, as the peasants, he felt, were the backbone of the nation, feeding that huge, vast population. Malcolm, of course, did not live long enough to see the changes that began to take place in the People's Republic of China within a decade later.

In Malcolm's last years, the United States was sending military advisors and specialists to Vietnam. Although the anti-Vietnam War movement had not quite begun to activate, Malcolm was aware of America's intentions to begin sending troops and take control of an area soon to become strategic for Western powers. Malcolm made the following prophetic statement: "Vietnam is the struggle of all third-world nations—the struggle against imperialism, colonialism, and neo-colonialism. Progressive people here must protest American incursion into Vietnam and Southeast Asia."

Malcolm's keen insight seemed to target all the critical areas of concern. Malcolm's astuteness, political theorizing, and principled thoughts were inspiring. He could lift what might have been obscure into clarity.

Malcolm, as a private individual, was as admirable as he was a political figure, leader, and teacher. He was a loving and caring husband and father. He exuded love for humanity and for the ordinary people on the street; the children and the elderly; but most of all for the most rejected, degraded, and ghettoized. He was unpretentious, sincere, genuine, and humble. After he returned from Mecca with the title El Hajj Malik Shabazz, his followers asked him, "What shall we call you now?" He responded, "What did you call me before?" They said, "Brother Malcolm." He answered, "Yes, just Brother Malcolm."

Conclusion: Racial Hierarchy and Ethnic Conflict in the United States

James Jennings

As black, Latino, and Asian people continue to numerically dominate many of the largest United States cities, it is important to ask,
as the contributors to this book have: What kinds of political
relationships will emerge among these groups? And, how will
these particular relationships mold or influence urban politics? The
chapters in this book show that relations among blacks, Latinos,
and Asians during the 1970s and 1980s and up to the current period
continue to reflect a mixed picture among these groups. In 1980
Miami experienced one of the worst urban riots since the 1960s. In
his chapter, Daryl Harris has suggested that conflict between blacks
and Cubans in Miami contributed to the rebellion in the black
community. Yet in this same city, the possibility of political alliances
between blacks and Cubans was illustrated a few months before
the riot when an "antibilingual" organization successfully pushed
an "English Only" referendum, banning the Dade County government from expending funds to translate public notices into Spanish. Some black leaders, and notably the NAACP, severely
criticized this measure as racist and supported Cuban efforts
against it.

In New York City divisive tensions between black and Puerto
Rican community activists were evident regarding questions of
controlling community action programs and organizations in some

neighborhoods during the 1960s. Yet, on the other hand, the community control movement in that city during the early 1970s clearly
represented a strong coalition among blacks, Puerto Ricans, and
Asians. Tensions between black and Puerto Rican political activists
erupted again in 1986 when a few black politicians endorsed a black
mayoral candidate, Herman Farrell, over a Puerto Rican candidate,
Herman Badillo. Yet just a few years later David Dinkins became
New York's first black mayor due, in large part, to Latino votes.[1] A
mixed picture is also evident in the political relations between black
and Asian communities. On one hand, derogatory statements
made about blacks by high-level Japanese government officials
and business leaders have contributed to deteriorating relations
between black and Asian communities. Yet at the same time Asian
activists in some cities have become key players in the development of rainbow coalitions that have been beneficial to black
electoral aspirants such as Jesse Jackson, Mel King in Boston, and
David Dinkins in New York City.[2]

RACIAL AND ETHNIC CONFLICT IN U.S. HISTORY

One could easily argue that racial and ethnic conflict is not new
for the cities of the United States. Ethnic conflict was not only a
significant characteristic of earlier urban life, but the conflict was
often accompanied by violence. Historian Richard Polenberg
points out that ethnicity, along with class and race, was a major
source of social differentiation in earlier periods; he argues that
"bad feelings between certain ethnic groups, never very far below
the surface in the best of times," erupted periodically.[3]

Today's racial and ethnic conflict differs from previous conflicts in that it exists between blacks, Latinos, and Asians, rather
than just between white ethnics and blacks or between various
white ethnic groups. Much of earlier racial and ethnic conflict,
furthermore, reflected either attempts on the part of blacks to
integrate or assimilate into white society and/or tensions between members of the white working class contesting control of
neighborhood boundaries and transition areas. Conflict surrounding neighborhood boundaries was more intensified, however, when it was racial, pitting blacks and whites against each
other. There have been numerous instances in U.S. history, as a
matter of fact, where white residents organized to stop blacks

from "moving in." Such resistance was even carried out violently when necessary.

In earlier periods racial and ethnic divisions were also apparent in the separation between suburbs and urban areas in the first decades of the twentieth century. The movement of white Anglo-Saxon Protestant groups into the suburbs was partially an attempt to flee the urban residential incursions of certain European ethnic groups. This resulted in a certain degree of ethnic cleavage between the suburban and urban areas, sometimes reflected in state legislatures resisting various efforts of urban governments.

Racial and ethnic conflict today increasingly involves groups of color living and working within the same neighborhood boundaries. The tensions that have been reported between blacks and Koreans in Los Angeles or New York City, for example, differ from those that existed in the struggles that ensued when blacks attempted to buy homes and integrate white parts of the city. In the latter case, whites perceived that blacks were invading their neighborhoods and schools, while the crucial issues dividing blacks and Koreans in this particular instance do not seem to involve control of residential areas and housing.

The conflict between earlier European ethnic groups and blacks also frequently involved competition for jobs. As Stephen Steinberg writes, "Beginning in the mid-nineteenth century, when blacks and Irish were locked in competition for jobs in New York and Boston, the feeling became rooted in the black community that immigrants were usurping opportunities that might otherwise have gone to them."[4] This belief was encouraged by black leaders like Booker T. Washington at the turn of the twentieth century as is evidenced in his famous speech "The Atlanta Compromise," delivered in 1895. To be sure, this belief did have a factual basis to it as is pointed out in works such as Harold X. Connolly's *A Ghetto Grows in Brooklyn*.[5] But today, when blacks boycott selected Korean stores in their communities, it is not clear that jobs are the only or even a major point of contention. It appears that cultural issues add to today's tensions. The black boycott of Korean stores in Brooklyn, New York, for example, while precipitated by incidents of violence, is also accompanied by behavior perceived "disrespectful" by blacks. Economic questions are certainly important as a factor determining the nature of relations between racial and ethnic groups, but the lack of cultural bridges between groups of color, as suggested by Karen Umemoto in her chapter, is also a problem.

In addition to the changing demography of cities, the economic transformation of the United States represents another important factor that is molding racial and ethnic conflict today, as is pointed out by Keith Jennings and Clarence Lusane. Demographic change is accompanied and exacerbated by a shrinking national economy. Up until the 1970s and 1980s racial and ethnic conflict erupted within a national economic framework that had been expanding, more or less, since the New Deal. The racial conflict did result in some degree of incorporation of a few blacks into the pluralist bargaining order, in part because the national economy could afford the addition of members of new groups. Today's racial and ethnic conflict, however, is erupting at a time when the national economy is much weaker than it was in earlier times, as is suggested by several contributors in this volume.

Prior to this latest stage of United States macroeconomic and national development, racial and ethnic conflict could at least be managed by allocating contending groups some piece of the nation's—or city's—economic pie. Today, in the context of a shrinking pie, this is not as easy to accomplish by political and economic leadership. Political bosses and mayors were able to funnel ethnic conflict into electoral channels, which allowed these politicians to function as unifying political symbols, thereby helping to overcome some of the social fragmentation of the city.[6] But party bosses were able to do this—to bargain and compromise in ways not threatening to the system—because economic growth allowed it. The lack of expendability in today's economy imposes on urban politicians a framework that limits the compromises associated with pluralist politics; this situation reflects Lester Thurow's "zero sum" politics where one group benefits or loses out—or perceives this to be the case—on the basis of the fortunes of other groups.[7]

RACIAL HIERARCHY AND ETHNIC CONFLICT

Various explanations or models have been offered to explain racial and ethnic conflict among blacks, Latinos, and Asians in cities today. In another article, I summarized these explanations in the literature as the "ethnic succession thesis," the "resentment thesis," the "job competition thesis," the "social and economic status thesis," and the "racial hierarchy thesis."[8] While more than one of these models has been touched upon in various chapters of this book, the one that is most commonly reflected here is the racial hierarchy model. Without using this term, sociologist Robert Blauner proposed this model when he explained that:

In a racial order a dominant group, which thinks of itself as distinct and superior, raises its social position by exploiting, controlling, and keeping down others who are categorized in racial or ethnic terms. When one or more groups are excluded from equal participation in society and from a fair share of its values, other groups not so excluded and dominated are correspondingly elevated in position. . . . Whether or not particular racist practices are followed consciously in order to benefit whites is not the issue. Whatever the intent, the system benefits all strata of the white population, at least in the short run—the lower and working classes as well as the middle and upper classes.[9]

Political scientist William E. Nelson utilizes a similar concept, though he does not call it racial hierarchy. He writes that United States society has a steadfast "racial nomenclature," with a caste-like quality. This racial nomenclature reflects the following characteristics: racial lines of demarcation maintain a system of privilege; social rules maintain the separation of blacks and whites; group membership in each category is lifelong; the basic philosophical boundaries of society have been defined by whites and for their benefit; the social system is only peripherally concerned with how blacks seek to define themselves in society; and very importantly, the system is renewed with the racial socialization of each new generation in the United States.[10]

Some time ago, Louis V. Kushnick specifically used the term "racial hierarchy" to explain how race has been employed as an impediment to white working-class consciousness in both the United States and Britain.[11] He argued that whites enjoyed psychological privileges and some material benefits as a bribe for not questioning a political economy slightly less exploitative of them, but more exploitative of blacks. The loyalty of poor and working-class whites is maintained, therefore, by assuring them that they would always have a higher social and economic status than blacks.

An explanation similar to Kushnick's is offered by Herman George, Jr., who writes that a racial subordination process is a fundamental reality in the United States with social, economic, cultural, and political implications. This process produces different kinds of access to social institutions and political power based on "whiteness."[12] David E. Hayes-Bautista explains how just the categorization or implication of "whiteness" conferred privileges for even a "nonwhite" group, like Mexicans: To be labeled Mexican was a disadvantage, while "to be labeled a Spaniard carried no social stigma." Hayes-Bautista continues, explaining: "There is a reason for this: Mexicans were Indians, dark, non-white, and considered uncivilized; Spanish were white, civilized, and European. In fact, until the last decade, the highest compliment an Anglo could pay a Mexican or Chicano was to call him or her 'Spanish' thereby conferring an honorary and temporary whiteness."[13] This development is supported by what Stephen Steinberg refers to as "occupational apartheid" meaning that "In the U.S. the essence of racial oppression is a racial division of labor, a system of occupational segregation that relegates most blacks to the least desirable jobs or that excludes them altogether from legitimate job markets."[14] Two recent works that also describe the entrenchment of the United States in racial hierarchy are Andrew Hacker's book *Two Nations: Black and White, Separate, Hostile, Unequal*, and Thomas B. Edsall and Mary A. Edsall's book *Chain Reaction: The Impact of Race, Rights, and Taxes on American Politics.*[15]

The above observations do suggest that U.S. society is characterized by a racial hierarchy that finds blacks continually occupying subdominant status relative to whites. In most arenas of social and economic interaction between blacks and whites, it is obvious that the latter are always on the top. And such status has been exploited by powerful interests to maintain the status quo. Blauner says:

White Americans enjoy special privilege in all areas of existence where racial minorities are systematically excluded or disadvantaged: housing and neighborhoods, education, income, and life style. Privilege is a relative matter, of course, but in racial and colonial systems it cannot be avoided, even by those who consciously reject the society and its privileges.[16]

Even a cursory examination of academe, entertainment and sports, housing, the military, management of cultural institutions, the corporate sector, or government in the United States reveals that generally blacks serve under, report to, or are held accountable by whites in power. And even in most of the institutions managed by blacks—whether historically black colleges, local social welfare programs, public schools, and other institutions—final authority rests with whites. As historian David R. Roediger has recently argued, this hierarchy has a long tradition in the United States. It is based, in part, on "whiteness" as privilege. Even the most economically depressed among the whites are privileged compared to blacks precisely due to their whiteness, according to Roediger, who says: "One might lose everything, but not whiteness."[17]

Racial hierarchy is related to another concept developed by sociologist Benjamin R. Ringer. He uses the term "duality" to describe how racial minorities have interacted with white society: "America's response to and treatment of its racial minorities have had a dual character that no single explanatory model can capture. This duality, we contend, is deeply rooted in America's past and is built into its structural and historical origins."[18]

Another observer proposes that the history of white ethnic mobility in the United States is based on this duality. Herman Block writes, "No matter how low any white ethnic group's social status was, it was usually higher than that of the Afro-Americans, with the former being given economic preference in the labor market. In other words, 'the newcomers from Europe had to be provided for,' even if it was to be at the expense of the indigenous colored American."[19]

Duality, like the term "racial hierarchy," can be described in terms of a social, economic, and cultural hierarchy that generally finds whites in dominant positions and status and blacks in sub-dominant status. While Ringer focuses on the social and historical origins of this social hierarchy and others may argue as to whether or not this arrangement has been intentionally constructed by certain forces and interests, the point is that it exists; whatever its origins and however the question of intent is resolved, the fact of the matter is that social life in the United States reflects a pervasive and persistent racial hierarchy.

The maintenance of this racial hierarchy, according to Steinberg, requires a system of control: "In a society organized on racist principles—that is, white domination and black subordination—

'racial harmony' depends on the routine maintenance of this hierarchical relationship. Since blacks have been less than content in this subordinate position, an elaborate system of controls has always been necessary to assure black compliance."[20] This is reiterated by Ringer:

The dominant white group has sought to impose a value-normative framework on relations between the races which would reaffirm its claim to superiority and keep the subordinated black group in its place. However, it has failed to gain the loyalty and acceptance of the blacks to this normative system and accordingly has had to rely heavily on force, coercion, and fraud to maintain its control over and it exploitation of the subordinated racial group for economic and political gain.[21]

Steinberg points out that earlier immigrant groups assisted in the racial subordination of blacks through hostility and violence: "The migration of blacks to northern cities and the rising level of racial protest have exacerbated the historic rivalry between immigrants and blacks. Wherever blacks went, it seemed that one or another ethnic group occupied the stratum just above them, and therefore black efforts for self-advancement tended to arouse ethnic loyalties and provoke an ethnic response."[22]

According to the racial hierarchy model, new ethnic groups coming to the United States today and competing with blacks for jobs, housing, and schools could also function to preserve a system of racial ordering for groups. There are some early signs that this may be happening with immigrants from former communist nations in Eastern Europe and the Soviet Union. As they and others arrive in the United States a socialization occurs that accommodates them into America's racial hierarchy. As pointed out by Russian writer Boris Kagarlitsky:

On Moscow TV, one can find the popular entertainer Yergienis Petrosian telling racist jokes that depict blacks as pre-verbal creatures sitting on tree branches. Now that the Soviet Union is a free country, it's just as forbidden to curse capitalism on TV as it once was to praise it—but if you want to poke a little fun at black people, that's another matter entirely.[23]

But European immigrants are not the only ones who might benefit from racial hierarchy in America. Columnist Jack Miles has suggested that in Los Angeles a system of racial, or at least ethnic, ordering operates to keep blacks unemployed, while it serves to treat Latinos slightly better by hiring them as servants. Miles writes:

 If you live here, you don't need the General Accounting Office to bring you the news. The almost total absence of black gardeners, bus boys, chamber maids, nannies, janitors, and construction workers in a city with a notoriously large pool of unemployed, unskilled black people leaps to the eye. . . . If the Latinos were not around to do that work, nonblack employers would be forced to hire blacks—but they'd rather not. They trust Latinos. They fear or disdain blacks. The result is unofficial but widespread preferential hiring of Latinos—the largest affirmative-action program in the nation, and one paid for, in effect, by blacks.[24]

The racial hierarchy model would predict, as suggested in the quotes by Miles and Kagarlitsky, that the treatment received by white immigrants coming into the United States today is qualitatively better than that meted to immigrants of color or even its own citizens of color. This is partially substantiated by a long-standing historical and racial pattern in the United States.

Blacks have been used as psychological, cultural, and even economic stepping-stones for the social and economic advancement of new groups. Support of this theory is also partially provided by sociologist Stanley Leiberson, when, in discussing the similarities and differences between the experiences of European immigrants to the United States and black migrants to the U.S. cities, he refers to the "Great Non-Sequitor."[25] Leiberson makes the point that while all new groups may have been the butt of jokes and stricken with poverty and various forms of social malaise at some point in their history in the United States, for European immigrants such reception was temporary, while for blacks, it is treatment that persists across generations.

Benjamin R. Ringer and Elinor R. Lawless show that despite initial settings of similar social and economic conditions, European immigrant communities could soon leapfrog over blacks for no other reason than that they were white—an important privilege in U.S. society. The Irish immigrants, for example, initially faced similar living conditions and competed with blacks for certain kinds of jobs; however, they soon gained the upper hand. By the 1850s, in places like New York and Boston, "they not only began to outnumber blacks, but even more importantly they soon learned and adopted the basic rules of the institutional game in the America of the day: the rights of the white man were superior to those of the black man in all of the institutional arenas of society."[26]

U.S. history provides a number of examples of white immigrant groups taking advantage of the nation's racial hierarchy:

By the time the white immigrant from Southern and Eastern Europe began to arrive in the late nineteenth and early twentieth century, the struggle had more or less been decided. These immigrants were the beneficiaries of the struggle that the Irish Catholics had waged earlier to establish the claim that even non-Protestant white immigrants had superior rights to those of the blacks, despite the fact that the latter had arrived in this country generations earlier.[27]

Ringer writes:

The process was repeated with each new wave of immigration. In each period the immigrants, most of whom had not previously been exposed to anti-black sentiments, quickly adopted these sentiments in the competitive struggle with blacks. Despite being victims of oppression themselves, they soon came to share with other white Americans the conviction that blacks were not the equal of any white and were, therefore, not entitled to the same rights and immunities as the whites in the social and economic Domain of the People.[28]

Some non-European immigrant groups, like the first wave of Cuban migration in the late 1950s and 1960s and some Asians, while not classified as white, are still able to take advantage of racial hierarchy and, therefore, may not question or challenge the resulting allocation of social and economic benefits. Even if the American dream does not work for them entirely, it may still be satisfying that at least it is more real for them than it is for blacks as a group. And being able to take advantage of society's racial hierarchy means that some nonwhite groups can have access to better housing, better schools, and broader economic opportunities than blacks in the United States.

Philip Kasinitz refers to this as "America's dilemma," and writes that:

New immigrants are pulled into the midst of the American dilemma almost immediately on arrival. Soviet emigres had scarcely begun to settle in Brooklyn before they were being referred to as the "the last white hope" by the area's real estate dealers, and some Asians seem to pick up American racial attitudes so quickly that one is reminded of a very bitter routine by Richard Pryor about Vietnamese refugees at citizenship class being taught the proper pronunciation of the word "nigger."[29]

Kasinitz adds that,

For Hispanics and black immigrants, who make up the majority of the new New Yorkers, relations with native blacks are deeply ambivalent, and matters are not helped when scholars use the relative gains of dark skinned immigrants to point up the alleged failures of native blacks and native ("New Yorican") Hispanics. For many such immigrants, the question of where they will fit in the city's racial division of power will depend largely on circumstances and on leadership. Many share the middle-class aspirations of most of the city's whites and blacks, and when these aspirations are merged with ethnic pride, many may indeed turn their backs on the underclass and head for the suburbs, psychologically if not physically.[30]

An illustration of how the existence of racial hierarchy has political implications for public policy is the case of the first wave of Cubans arriving in the United States in the early 1960s. As is pointed out by sociologists Candace Nelson and Marta Tienda, Cubans were "primarily political refugees rather than economic migrants. Their reception in this country was not the tacit acceptance by employers hungry for cheap labor, but rather a public welcome by the Federal government eager to harbor the heroic victims of a communist dictatorship."[31] One example of this public welcome is the Cuban Refugee Act of 1961; this law provided extensive and easy credit to Cuban entrepreneurs in New York state in the 1960s. According to Daryl Harris in Chapter 6 and others, U.S. government programs provided about $1 billion of refugee assistance to Cubans fleeing the Castro regime during the 1960s.[32] Thus, despite the ongoing struggle of blacks for these same kinds of benefits, one had to be Cuban in order to receive this government assistance. While Cubans might face discrimination from whites, they at least enjoyed government benefits not available to the black community.

Many small businesses were started under Cuban ownership due to the credit available through the Cuban Refugee Act. Puerto Ricans, on the other hand, were not eligible to receive this kind of credit and, therefore, had a more difficult time in starting small business ventures. For blacks, eligibility for this kind of governmental resource was completely out of the question. This situation may partially explain the sense of political solidarity that periodically arises between blacks and Puerto Ricans in places like New York City and Chicago.

Another example of the effect of racial hierarchy has been the institutional response to the idea of "reparations" as a way of responding to historical injustices against various groups. The general reaction to demands for reparations on the part of black activists has been much more negative than it has been for other groups. This contrasts with the official government response to the Japanese American community regarding reparations for the internment of this community during World War II. It also contrasts with the general acceptance of the idea that Jewish victims of the Holocaust should be compensated in some way by Germany or with efforts to provide reparations to Native Americans for treaties that were illegally made or ignored between earlier white settlers and their local governments and various tribes.[33] Claims by blacks that the U.S. government should also provide that community with reparations for past injustices, however, have many times been met with incredulity and ridicule.

These examples are mentioned in order to propose that the continuing existence of a racial hierarchy in the United States, where symbolically and substantively blacks generally occupy the bottom and whites the top of the social and economic scale, will serve as fuel to flame racial and ethnic divisions among communities of color. On the other hand, building a politics that confronts racial hierarchy but that goes beyond "mere racial identity" politics, as suggested by Manning Marable, Daniel Osuna, Yuri Kochiyama, and other contributors, may generate collaboration among communities of color. This collaboration, in turn, may be what is needed in urban America to revitalize a movement of fundamental political change directed at democratizing our society and ensuring social justice.

NOTES

This chapter is an updated version of "New Urban Racial and Ethnic Conflicts in U.S. Politics," *Sage Race Relations Abstracts*, vol. 17, no. 3 (August 1992).

1. See Angelo Falcon, "Black and Latino Politics in New York City: Race and Ethnicity in a Changing Urban Context," in F. C. Garcia, ed., *Latinos and the Political System* (Indianapolis: University of Notre Dame Press, 1988); Charles Green and Basil Wilson, *The Struggle for Black Empowerment in New York City* (New York: Praeger, 1989); and Ralph C. Gomes and Linda Faye Williams, eds., *From Exclusion to Inclusion: The Long Struggle for African American Political Power* (Westport, Conn.: Greenwood, 1992).

2. For an example of this in Boston, see Michael Liu, "Grass Roots Politics and Boston's Asian Communities," *Radical America*, vol. 17, no. 6 and vol. 18, no. 1 (May 1984).

3. Richard Polenberg, *One Nation Divisible: Class, Race, and Ethnicity in the United States Since 1938* (New York: Penguin Books, 1981), p. 40.

4. Stephen Steinberg, *The Ethnic Myth: Race, Ethnicity and Class in America* (Boston: Beacon Press, 1981), p. 202.

5. Harold X. Connolly, *A Ghetto Grows in Brooklyn* (New York: New York University Press, 1977).

6. Judd O. Robertson, *American Myth, American Reality* (New York: Hill & Wang, 1980), p. 238.

7. Lester Thurow, *The Zero-Sum Society* (New York: Viking Penguin, 1981), p. 17.

8. Yet another model, the "frontier-contact" explanation for ethnic conflict was developed by sociologist Hubert M. Blalock, Jr. This model may not be appropriate for explaining urban conflict in America, however, because its focus is on the colonization efforts of white Europeans directed at "simple hunting and gathering bands or with cultures at the hoe-agriculture level of development." Herbert M. Blalock, Jr., *Toward a Theory of Minority Group Relations* (New York: John Wiley and Sons, 1967), p. 76; see James Jennings, "New Urban Racial and Ethnic Conflicts in United States Politics," *Sage Race Relations Abstracts*, vol. 17, no. 3 (August 1992).

9. Robert Blauner, *Racial Oppression in America* (New York: Harper and Row, 1972), p. 22.

10. William E. Nelson, "Racial Definition: Background for Divergence," *Phylon*, vol. 47, no. 4, (December 1986).

11. Louis V. Kushnick, "Racism and Class Consciousness in Modern Capitalism," in B. Bowser and R. G. Hunt, eds., *Impact of Racism on White America* (Beverly Hills, Calif.: Sage, 1981), pp. 191–216.

"12. Herman George, Jr., "Black America, The 'Underclass' and the Subordination Process," *Black Scholar*, vol. 19, no. 3 (May/June 1988), p. 48.

13. David E. Hayes-Bautista, "Identifying Hispanic Populations: The Influence of Research Methodology Upon Public Policy," *American Journal of Public Health*, vol. 70, no. 4 (April 1980), p. 354.

14. Stephen Steinberg, "Occupational Segregation," *The Nation*, vol. 253, no. 20 (December 9, 1991), p. 744.

15. Andrew Hacker, *Two Nations: Black and White, Separate, Hostile, Unequal* (New York: Charles Scribner's Sons, 1992); T. B. Edsall and M. A. Edsall, *Chain Reaction: The Impact of Race, Rights, and Taxes on American Politics* (New York: W. W. Norton, 1991).

16. Blauner, op. cit., p. 23.

17. David R. Roediger, *The Wages of Whiteness: Race and the Making of the American Working Class* (London: Verso, 1991), p. 61.

18. Benjamin R. Ringer, *We the People: Duality and America's Treatment of Its Racial Minorities* (London: Tavistock, 1983), p. 7.

19. Herman D. Block, *The Circle of Discrimination: An Economic and Social Study of the Black Man in New York* (New York: New York University Press, 1969), p. 37.

20. Steinberg, *The Ethnic Myth*, p. 211.

21. Ringer, op. cit., p. 237.

22. Steinberg, *The Ethnic Myth*, p. 218.

23. Boris Kagarlitsky, "Back in the USA," *Social Justice*, vol. 18, nos. 1–2 (1991), p. 29.

24. Jack Miles, "Immigration and the New American Dilemma: Blacks vs. Browns," *The Atlantic*, vol. 27, no. 4 (October 1992), p. 53.

25. Stanley Leiberson, *A Piece of the Pie: Blacks and White Immigrants Since 1880* (Berkeley: University of California Press, 1980), pp. 363–384.

26. Benjamin R. Ringer and Elinor R. Lawless, *Race, Ethnicity and Society* (New York: Routledge, 1989), p. 203.

27. Ibid., p. 204.

28. Ibid., p. 266.

29. Philip Kasinitz, "The City's New Immigrants," *Dissent* (Fall 1987), p. 504.

30. Ibid., p. 505.

31. Candace Nelson and Marta Tienda, "The Structure of Hispanic Ethnicity," in R. D. Alba, ed., *Ethnicity and Race in the USA: Toward the Twenty-First Century*. (New York: Routledge, 1989), p. 58.

32. "Browns vs. Blacks," *Time* (July 29, 1991); see also F. Padilla, *Latino Ethnic Consciousness: Case of Puerto Ricans and Mexicans in Chicago* (Indian-

apolis: University of Notre Dame Press, 1985); also, S. Pedraza-Bailey, *Political and Economic Migrants in America: Cubans and Mexicans* (Austin: University of Texas Press, 1985).

33. See Richard F. America, *Paying the Social Debt: What White America Owes Black America* (Westport, Conn.: Praeger, 1993).

For Further Reading

Bach, Robert. *Changing Relations: Newcomers and Established Residents in U.S. Communities.* New York: Ford Foundation, 1993.

Blalock, Hubert M. *Toward a Theory of Minority-Group Relations.* New York: John Wiley & Sons, 1967.

Bouvier, Leon F., and Robert W. Gardner. *Immigration to the United States: The Unfinished Story* 41, no. 4 (November 1986). Washington, D.C.: Population Reference Bureau.

Browning, Rufus P., Dale R. Marshall, and David H. Tabb. *Protest Is Not Enough.* Berkeley: University of California Press, 1984.

_____ *Racial Politics in American Cities.* New York: Longman, 1990.

Day, Barbara, "New York: David Dinkins Opens the Door," in Mike Davis, Steven Hiatt, Marie Kennedy, Susan Ruddick, and Michael Sprinker, eds., *Fire in the Hearth.* London: Verso, 1990.

Eisinger, Peter K. *Politics and Displacement: Racial and Ethnic Transition in Three American Cities.* New York: Academic, 1980.

Erie, Steven. "Rainbow's End: From the Old to the New Urban Ethnic Politics," in Lionel Maldonaldo and Joan Moore, eds., *Urban Ethnicity in the United States: New Immigrants and Old Minorities.* Beverly Hills, Calif.: Sage, 1985.

Falcon, A. "Black and Latino Politics in New York City: Race and Ethnicity in a Changing Urban Context," in F. Chris Garcia, ed., *Latinos in the Political System.* Indianapolis: University of Notre Dame Press, 1988.

Gomes, Ralph C., and Linda Faye Williams, eds. *From Exclusion to Inclusion: The Long Struggle for African American Political Power.* Westport, Conn.: Greenwood, 1992.

Green, Charles, and Basil Wilson. *The Struggle for Black Empowerment in New York City.* New York: Praeger, 1989.

Hahn, Harlan, and Timothy Almy. "Ethnic Politics and Racial Issues: Voting in Los Angeles." *Western Political Quarterly* 24 (1971): 719–730.

Hahn, Harlan, D. Klingman, and H. Pachon. "Candidate: The Los Angeles Mayoralty Elections of 1969 and 1973," in H. Hahn and C. Levine, eds., *Urban Politics.* New York: Longman, 1980.

Henry, Charles P. "Black-Chicano Coalitions: Possibilities and Problems." *Western Journal of Black Studies* 4 (1980): 222–232.

Hero, Rodney E. "Multiracial Coalitions in City Elections Involving Minority Candidates: Some Evidence from Denver." *Urban Affairs Quarterly* 25, no. 2 (December 1989).

Hutchinson, E. O. "Obstacles to Unity Multiply for Blacks and Latinos," *Los Angeles Times* (10 September 1991).

Jennings, James. "Blacks and Latinos in the American City in the 1990s: Toward Political Alliance or Social Conflict." *The National Political Science Review* 3 (1992).

———. "New Urban Racial and Ethnic Conflicts in U.S. Politics." *Sage Race Relations Abstracts* 17, no. 3 (August 1992).

Kasarda, John D. "Urban Change and Minority Opportunities," in P. E. Peterson, ed., *The New Urban Reality.* Washington, D.C.: Brookings Institution, 1985.

Liu, Michael. "Grass Roots Politics and Boston's Asian Communities." *Radical America* 17, no. 6 and 18, no. 1 (May 1984).

McClain, Paula D., and Albert K. Karnig. "Black and Hispanic Socioeconomic and Political Competition." *American Political Science Review* 84, no. 2 (June 1990): 536–545.

Mladenka, Kenneth R. "Blacks and Hispanics in Urban Politics." *American Political Science Review* 83, no. 1 (March 1989): 167–191.

Mohl, Raymond A. "Race, Ethnicity, and Urban Politics in the Miami Metropolitan Area." *Florida Environmental and Urban Issues* 3 (1982): 1–6, 23–25.

Moynihan, Daniel P. "Patterns of Ethnic Succession: Blacks and Hispanics in New York City." *Political Science Quarterly* 94, no. 1 (Spring 1979).

Moynihan, Daniel P., and N. Glazer. *Beyond the Melting Pot.* Cambridge, Mass.: MIT Press, 1970.

Nelson, C., and M. Tienda,"The Structure of Hispanic Ethnicity," in R. D. Alba, ed., *The Ethnicity and Race in the USA: Toward the Twenty-First Century*. New York: Routledge, 1989.

O'Hare, William P. *America's Minorities: The Demographics of Diversity* 47, no. 4. Washington, D.C.: Population Reference Bureau, December 1992.

O'Hare, William P., and Judy C. Felt. *Asian Americans: America's Fastest Growing Minority Group*, no. 19. Washington, D.C.: Population Reference Bureau, February 1991.

O'Hare, William P., Kelvin M. Pollard, Taynis L. Mann, and Mary M. Kent. *African Americans in the 1990s* 46, no. 1. Washington, D.C.: Population Reference Bureau, July 1991.

Oliver, Melvin L., and James H. Johnson, Jr. "Interethnic Conflict in an Urban Ghetto: The Case of Blacks and Latinos in Los Angeles." *Social Movements, Conflicts, and Change* 6 (1984): 57–94.

Padilla, F. *Latino Ethnic Consciousness: The Case of Puerto Ricans and Mexicans in Chicago*. Indianapolis: University of Notre Dame Press, 1985.

Pedraza-Bailey, S. *Political and Economic Migrants in America: Cubans and Mexicans*. Austin: University of Texas Press, 1985.

Pickney, Alphonso. "Prejudice toward Mexican and Negro Americans," in John H. Burma, ed., *Mexicans in the United States*. Cambridge, Mass.: Schenkman, 1970.

Prud'homme, A. "Blacks vs. Browns," *Time* (29 July 1991).

Sowell, Thomas. *Ethnic America: A History*. New York: Basic Books, 1981.

Steinberg, Stephen. *The Ethnic Myth: Race, Ethnicity and Class in America*. Boston: Beacon, 1981.

Tchen, J. Kuo Wei. "The Chinatown-Harlem Initiative: Building Multicultural Understanding in New York City," in J. Brecher and T. Costello, eds., *Building Bridges: The Emerging Grassroots Coalition of Labor and Community*. New York: Monthly Review, 1990.

The Trotter Review 7, no. 2 (Fall 1993). Special issue on the political and social relations between communities of color. Boston: William Monroe Trotter Institute, University of Massachusetts Boston.

Valdivieso, Rafael, and Cary Davis. *U.S. Hispanics: Challenging Issues for the 1990s*, no. 17. Washington, D.C.: Population Reference Bureau, December 1988.

Yun, Grace. *Intergroup Cooperation in Cities: African, Asian, and Hispanic American Communities*. New York: Asian-American Federation of New York, 1993.

Index

About the Contributors

DARYL HARRIS teaches at the University of Connecticut, Storrs. His areas of focus include black politics and urban politics. His doctoral dissertation is a study of black urban violence in Miami during the 1980s.

CHARLES P. HENRY is Associate Professor of Afro-American Studies at the University of California, Berkeley. He is the author of *Culture and African American Politics* and *The Search for Common Ground: Jesse Jackson's Campaign for President*.

JAMES JENNINGS is Professor of Political Science and Director of the William Monroe Trotter Institute at the University of Massachusetts at Boston. His books include *The Politics of Black Empowerment; Race, Politics, and Economic Development: Community Perspectives; and Understanding the Nature of Poverty in Urban America*. He is also involved in a broad range of civic and neighborhood activism in black and Puerto Rican communities.

KEITH JENNINGS is an activist who has lectured in many countries around the world on issues of race, peace, and human rights.

He is currently working in Washington, D.C., with the Council on Churches.

YURI KOCHIYAMA is a long-time community activist in Harlem. She has served on the boards of Third World Media News (1972–73); Committee for Puerto Rican Decolonization (1973–74); and the New Harlem YWCA (1976–77); and on the Steering Committee of Women and Law Conference (1984–86).

CLARENCE LUSANE is an author, activist, and journalist in Washington, D.C. For more than twenty years, he has written about and been active in national black politics, U.S. foreign policy, and social issues such as education and drugs. One of his books, *Pipe Dream Blues: Racism and the War on Drugs*, analyzes the historic and contemporary relationship between drugs and racism.

MANNING MARABLE is Professor of History and Political Science and Director of the Institute for Research in African American Studies at Columbia University in New York City. Dr. Marable has chaired African American Studies departments at Colgate University and Ohio State University, and from 1989 to 1993 he was Professor of History and Political Science at the University of Colorado at Boulder. Dr. Marable is the author of several books, including *Black American Politics* and *W.E.B. Du Bois: Black Radical Democrat*.

DANIEL OSUNA is the International Secretary of El Partido de La Raza Unida, based in Phoenix, Arizona. He has worked extensively in organizing students, youth, and gangs in communities of color in the southwestern United States.

JUANITA TAMAYO LOTT is president of Tamayo Lott Associates, a public policy consulting firm in Silver Spring, Maryland. She is also a contributing editor for the *Asian American Almanac* and a senior research associate of the National Academy of Sciences. Ms. Lott advises a variety of federal agencies, nonprofit agencies, and school systems. Her publications and lectures focus on the implications of demographic changes, race, ethnicity, and gender.

KAREN UMEMOTO is a doctoral candidate in the Department of Urban Studies and Planning, Massachusetts Institute of Technology. She is one of the cofounders of the 1984 Los Angeles Rainbow Coaltion. She has worked extensively on a broad range of issues in Asian communities in Boston and Los Angeles.